T0161041

Down and Out in England and Italy

Down and Out in England and Italy

Alberto Prunetti

Translated from the Italian by Elena Pala

SCRIBE
Melbourne • London

Scribe Publications
2 John St, Clerkenwell, London WC1N 2ES, United Kingdom
18–20 Edward St, Brunswick, Victoria 3056, Australia
3754 Pleasant Ave, Suite 100, Minneapolis, Minnesota 55409, USA

Published by Scribe 2021

Typeset in Adobe Caslon by the publishers

Printed and bound in the UK by CPI Group (UK) Ltd, Croydon CR0 4YY

Scribe is committed to the sustainable use of natural resources and the use
of paper products made responsibly from those resources.

978 1 913348 37 3 (UK edition)
978 1 922310 61 3 (Australian edition)
978 1 950354 85 6 (US edition)
978 1 922586 16 2 (ebook)

Catalogue records for this book are available from the National Library of
Australia and the British Library.

This book has been translated thanks to a translation grant awarded by the
Italian Ministry of Foreign Affairs and International Cooperation.
*Questo libro è stato tradotto grazie a un contributo alla traduzione assegnato dal
Ministero degli Affari Esteri e della Cooperazione Internazionale italiano.*

scribepublications.co.uk
scribepublications.com.au
scribepublications.com

to those who worked the night shifts
to build 108-metre-long steel tracks

to those who left home to study
travelling on those very same steel tracks

to Abd Elsalam Ahmed Eldanf
who died on the picket line

Nearly all the incidents described there actually happened, though they have been rearranged.

George Orwell, *The Road to Wigan Pier*

Well, sir, I thought I had only found a cook, but it was a crew I had discovered. Between Silver and myself we got together in a few days a company of the toughest old salts imaginable — not pretty to look at, but fellows, by their faces, of the most indomitable spirit. I declare we could fight a frigate.

Robert Louis Stevenson, *Treasure Island*

Us poor people are not suited to tragedy, tragedy is for kings and princes and other such aristocratic folk. Comedy — the ridiculing of pain — better befits us lowly commoners, and, in some illustrious cases, our deeds are the stuff of epics. Comedy is better suited to the enterprising stratagems we resort to in order to survive.

Luigi Di Ruscio,
La neve nera di Oslo (The Black Snow of Oslo)

Disclaimer

This is a work of autobiographical fiction. Names, characters, businesses, places, and events are either the products of the author's imagination or used in a fictitious manner. Any resemblance to actual persons, living or dead, or actual events is purely coincidental.

Sort of.

The oath

We the cooks of the United Kingdom solemnly swear before Her Majesty the Queen to fight the infamous pathogenic bacteria, given to all manner of viciousness and capable of inducing the most grievous bouts of nausea and vomiting. We will deny *Clostridium perfringens* access to the British soil — that ghastly, degenerate agitator that creeps into restaurants and can count on the logistical support of *botulinum*. The fearsome *Staphylococcus aureus* — devious bowel terrorist — will be pushed back across the Channel, together with the so-called European *Bacillus cereus*, which causes abdominal pain and spasms as well as nefarious bouts of bloating. As loyal subjects of the Crown, we swear this oath on our rolling pins and vow to eradicate *E. coli* and *Campylobacter* from every plate — migrant bacteria that infiltrate the body of unwitting British ingesters and, after a four-day incubation period, produce tragic effects, thus jeopardising the reputation of Great British kitchens.

God Save the Queen. Having spoken these words, I'd never felt more British.

With this oath, my training course came to an end. The five-hour seminar had earned me the 'Food and Health Certificate', a prestigious academic qualification that is bestowed by law upon any hospitality worker who is required to handle or serve food in the UK, from skivvies to maître d's.

Those were dark times. The barometer forecast imminent storms. Distrust and poverty were on the rise, as were xenophobia and general gloom. The winds of resentment blew, scattering about victim mentality, imperial nostalgia, and terror-related anxiety like empty cans on the streets. Great British Kitchens up and down the Kingdom were preparing for a fight to the death. I, too, was ready to jump into the fray, but our ranks were made up of not-so-patriotic crackpots. A wandering pleb, I had joined the SKANK (Stonebridge Kitchen Assistant Nasty Kommittee), the most disreputable gang of rogue cooks you'd ever had the pleasure of coming across. Congratulations — we'd tell our employers to their faces — you're paying minimum wage for the finest bunch of ruffians ever to dish out slop in school canteens on behalf of Her Majesty Queen Elizabeth, second of her name.

Aside from your humble narrator, others you'd find ladling out fodder included a violent hooligan and a fence, supported by a car thief who got arrested with his apron still on. All aged between twenty and thirty, all sturdy British working-class offspring with no prospects, pin-balling between social services and unemployment benefits. Then there was Gerald, my favourite, who together with me (a working-class university graduate fleeing zero-hour contracts in Italy) made up the 'learned' part of the gang.

Gerald was a seventy-year-old former radio actor who worshipped Shakespeare. After a brain injury he'd started working in school kitchens, where he enjoyed frightening pupils. To do this, he used a carefully refined theatrical technique: as he served starchy, cement-like potato soup, ladle in hand, he'd reply to the inevitable 'thank yous' from well-behaved pupils with a 'pleasure, my pleeeeasuuuure' in an ogre's voice, while drops of sweat ran off his thick brows and plopped into the trays of hot goop, producing circular waves. He stank like an old goat and wore the same T-shirt for months, adorned with crusty sweat rings and embellished with oil stains and Bolognaise blotches like a Holy Shroud.

It's him I find myself thinking of from time to time: greetings to you, Gerald, great artist, who knew *Hamlet* by heart, sang Rossini, and upset adults and children with glee. What a team we were. Experts in all culinary arts, we distinguished ourselves through our unauthorised absences, misconduct, and incompetence, and did ourselves proud in our lack of application too. Some of us favoured theft, but we all excelled at fighting and serious damage to company property. As for our brand image, we were poster boys for dishonesty and intoxication by means of drink, and in terms of public relations, clients and suppliers could always count on our violent, dangerous, and intimidating conduct.

What a crew, what a pack of reprobates! Scoundrels of

the world, unite! Ross, Ian, Gerald, Tim, and Fatty Boy. And Silver too, the smuggler cook. Ahoy! And then came Rodrigo, the hyperactive British-Ecuadorian pizza chef's assistant, and Brian, the toilet cleaner from Bristol — an esteemed mentor in the art of unclogging blocked crappers with his bare hands.

Such was the cast of outsized characters amongst whom I found myself in my glorious journey through the UK. All were working-class heroes with whom I played football, leafed through borderline pornographic tabloids, and cleaned bogs between one sacking and the next, pursued by inner demons and *The Sun*'s Euro-bashing headlines as I tried to make an honest living as a humble servant of the Crown.

I swore an oath. God Save the Queen.

And those who enter the Kingdom shall keep the toilets clean.

Of course I do

Then the grand turmoil of the day started — the dinner hour. I wish I could be Zola for a little while, just to describe that dinner hour.

George Orwell, *Down and Out in Paris and London*

Margherita, the pizza named after Margaret Thatcher.

Margherita, the pizza named after Margaret Thatcher.

Margherita, the pizza named after Margaret Thatcher.

I kept repeating this stupid mantra — thus disrespecting Italy's Queen Margherita, robbed of her title — in the hope that the Iron Lady's ghost would rise from the depths of the eighth circle of Hell to grant a young Italian immigrant's wish: finding a job in the UK.

By then, I had knocked on the door of five Italian pizzerias in Bristol's city centre. I had to go cap in hand to Italian restaurants because my English was ridiculous. I sounded like an automaton. If I wanted to tell someone they were lucky, I'd say, 'You've seen a nice world', a word-by-word translation of a popular saying from the town of Livorno. And if anyone gave me a funny look, I'd respond with the wise Tuscan adage, 'How wish to drink eggs' (meaning, 'You've got to drink a few

eggs still and grow up before you can look me in the eye.').
Understandably, when I asked a question, English speakers
looked right through me as if I didn't exist. I spoke like Google
Translate and no one could understand me.

Suffering as I was from this communication block, I
thought I'd better 'touch iron' — quite literally — when it
came to asking for a job. In Italy, iron is a good-luck charm
and a little superstition doesn't cost anything. But where
could I find a proper sheet of iron like the ones forged in the
steelworks in my native Piombino, untarnished, hot- and cold-
tempered, hardened in oil and diesel, and trimmed with a wire
brush grinder? The only piece of iron that came to mind was
Thatcher — the Iron Lady herself.

Had I been more familiar with British culture, I would
have touched wood, never iron, to invoke Lady Luck. But
alas, Baroness Thatcher didn't bring good luck, and perhaps
her ghost took my ironic conjuring as a challenge, for I would
soon come to suspect that my blasphemous prayer had invoked
something more sinister … Was it possible that, unbeknown to
me, I had unleashed the evil forces that oppressed the British
working class?

I did, eventually, find work. Clad in white — a ceremonial
colour that rather suits me — I reported for duty. The boss, an
old lady from Salerno whose family had emigrated to the UK
in the sixties, formally pronounced me a pizza chef. She made
me bow my head, and standing on her tiptoes she secured a
blue handkerchief around my neck: the ritual reminded me
of a feudal investiture, which didn't surprise me since the

monarchy was alive and well in Britain. As for her husband, he was from the Veneto region and had arrived in the UK in the eighties. On my first day, he told me stories about his time in the National Service back home — other than that, he only really piped up after a bottle of Prosecco. His English was mediocre, but still better than mine.

Where I worked, English wasn't actually spoken at all: aside from the waiters, who were British, the kitchen staff were all Italian or Latin American. I had to learn the waiters' names so I could call them when the pizzas came out of the oven just as they had to learn the menu by heart, and that was the extent of our communication. These four walls I now called home were partitioned into various spaces: there were the storeroom and kitchen — a Purgatory of unhappiness and second-degree burns; next door was the pizza oven — my very own prison cell, barely measuring 4 m² and with an average registered temperature of 400 degrees Celsius; and of course the dining room, where customers sat stuffing their stomachs as waiters relentlessly shuttled back and forth.

The room next to the toilets had been furnished as a poky little bedroom, crammed full of plush toys and porcelain dolls; it was meant as a convalescing space, as it were, for the waitresses, who would often faint in the line of duty. Besides the disquieting legions of teddy bears, that creepy snug also contained a small bookcase displaying cooking magazines and a collection of racist propaganda books in the noble language of Dante, fiercely proclaiming the superiority of the Mediterranean cuisine over all others.

The sleeping quarters for all the non-British kitchen staff, including yours truly, were on the first floor; the cost of accommodation was deducted from our wages. Said wages were, in theory, fairly decent compared to those of my illustrious country, but once stripped of all the food, accommodation and other unspecified legal costs, my salary actually amounted to less than minimum wage, which at the time was six pounds fifty per hour.

'Capricciosa: tomato mushrooms olives ham artichokes mozzarella ... done! In the oven! They've got a nerve ... yes, *signora*, almost ready, I'm just turning it — here you go! Liza! Will you take this bloody pizza away, *cazzo*! God I want to die ... all right sì sì coming! Helloooo? The fuck you looking at? This one had oregano? So write it in the fucking order will you? How many to take out? Here ... you ... fucking ... go ... Liza! Anchovies capers mozzarella ... in the oven! The dough's too thick you say, boss? Not as thick as you though. Yes, *signora*, how may I help ... A pepperoni with extra toppings? *Sì, signora* ... all right, all right, coming up ... My face blank, my brain off ... is this the real life is this just fantasy? I'm not working I'm just moving ... speed is all I need ... *vaffanculo* ... it never ends ... in the oven! Liza! Come and get this bloody pizza, it's stone cold ...'

This is an immigrant pizza chef's stream of consciousness. Repeat it for ten hours a day, seven days a week, four weeks a month, and you'll win a job in an Italian restaurant in the

UK. My responsibilities included: preparing and lining up the tubs with all the various condiments and toppings; making the dough; keeping the oven hot; rolling the dough; sprinkling the toppings on the pizzas, and popping them in the oven for the one hundred and fifty customers who ate at the restaurant daily, both lunch and dinner. Then I had to clean everything up and go straight to bed avoiding any distractions, and specifically any contact with the British staff who — according to the *padrone* — were all arrogant and spoilt and had preposterous demands such as employment contracts. Not us though, we didn't need contracts, because 'we Italians are honest people, and our word is our bond'. And we were all 'a big happy family'. And we were all in the same boat, cross my heart and hope to die.

Speaking of boats, to escape the monotony of work I'd asked the main chef to teach me to tie knots: half-English, half-god knows what, citizen of the world and stranger in every country, the chef, John Silver, was a reformed sea dog, meaning he'd sailed all over the world from the Caribbean to Madagascar, until an ill-fated current (and a serious work accident that left him lame in one leg) landed him on the shores of the Channel. Now a refugee in a Bristol restaurant kitchen, the closest he got to the sea was seasoning fish. He was a buccaneer who had a girl in every port until life's various misfortunes left him stranded, weary, and disillusioned.

He spoke all the languages of the world and readily combined them in every sentence. He might start in Spanish, then move on to Italian, often with an English expletive thrown in for good measure: 'Necesito a fucking day off, capeesh?' He was as old as the hills. His long white hair fell in matted clumps over the big gold hoops dangling from his ears, and faded, barely visible tattoos covered his leathery arms, criss-crossed by a maze of protruding veins.

Silver was a true knot virtuoso: 'Leave this end of the corda longer, put a finger over it like that. Now, loop the corda round your finger, then between your finger and the other end, and pull. Dále, cabròn! Eso! Bravo!' And, hey presto, the rope slid effortlessly in and out.

Just as effortlessly, however, the *signora* would spot us loitering outside the back door, thick as thieves, Silver smoking his blond tobacco and coughing his lungs up as he supervised my knot training. 'Idle hands do the devil's work' — she'd chide — 'as these Brits know all too well, these slackers who live on benefits! Nice gravy train they've hopped on … paid to do nothing! It beggars belief … This country's like treasure island to them!' she'd say. At the mention of *Treasure Island*, Silver would briefly prick up his ears, then go back to chopping onions.

I was curious about the benefits system, this mysterious welfare mechanism the boss was very reluctant to explain. 'We Italians would do well to stay away from those pasty-faced scroungers altogether,' she continued. 'Hooligans. Riff-raff,' she said. 'Ruffians. Troublemakers. Back home in Italy they'd lock them up and throw away the key!' God forbid we fraternised with these barbarians.

It's not like we lacked company anyway — her husband was all too happy to entertain us — such an honour! At his second bottle of Prosecco, he would come upstairs and pay us a visit in our dorm, usually during our break between the lunch and dinner shifts, around 4 pm. The old geezer would wax lyrical about his teenage escapades back home, singing the praises of tender young flesh — 'Ah, those were the days!' Needless to say, putting up with this moron's booze-fuelled strolls down memory lane didn't earn us any extra pay.

They were an odd couple, our bosses. The wife assuaged her ill-concealed inferiority complex towards the British by reading cooking magazines ('The Mediterranean cuisine is number one in the world; Britain has no culinary tradition!'), while the husband — when he was sober — was a real machinery fanatic, a gadgetry fetishist who got off on stuff like the delicate friction of ball bearings in the mozzarella grinder. He was, however, frequently drunk, and on such occasions he would regale us with popular sayings from his native Padua ('Chicken soup and red wine and like a king you'll dine!') while myself and another guy from Naples exchanged puzzled looks.

Unlike her husband, the wife was a pragmatic type who didn't indulge in any frivolous pastimes, the only exception being a peculiar accounting ritual of hers. Her most perverse passion, in fact, consisted in recording in her notebook how many customers had dined at the restaurant on any given day, then comparing it to the same day the year before. Rejoicing in the slimmest uptick in footfall, she'd then attempt to estimate how many people would come the following day, and warn the staff that they'd have to work just as hard. 'We're expecting around three hundred tomorrow,' she'd say, and I'd touch iron, wood — anything within reach really — to ward off such an ominous prospect.

Usually, however, her forecast spanned a broad interval, like the highest and lowest points on a parabolic curve: 'Tomorrow could be anywhere between seven and three hundred!' No shit, Sherlock. She reminded me of an SS guard ('tomorrow we'll gas between three and three thousand, we'll play it by ear') or of a maths teacher with her blackboard. To her, numbers were nothing short of miraculous, and she was very pleased with herself for convincing her son to study statistics at Bristol's prestigious university — he, apparently, was allowed to fraternise with the English — because numbers don't lie, two and two is four, a bird in hand is worth two in the bush, got to bring home the bacon, etc.

Speaking of animal fats, I couldn't understand why the meaty pasta sauce we know as 'ragù' in Italy is called 'Bolognaise' in the UK. In the twenty or so years of my life prior to moving to the UK I'd never set foot outside my native Tuscany, and I thought everyone on planet Earth ate pasta the same way. It was in that Bristol kitchen that I learnt, from Silver (an expert in culinary history as well as Italian immigration), that before olive oil became widely available, first-generation Italian immigrants in the UK would fry onions in lard, like they used to do in Bologna.

Besides, said Silver, leaning on his crutch, 'down in the South of Italy se hace el ragù à la napolitaine, n'est-ce pas? They make ragù with whole chunks of meat, not mince like in Bologna, capeesh?' He stuffed his long white hair inside his chef's hat and continued, in his strange mongrel vernacular: 'For the soffritto, primero la cebolla — onion first. You put it in the pan until it looks like gold.' 'Like gold?' 'Mais oui, bien sûr, il faut la faire revenir. Then you add bacon and involtini and pork sossages and meatboals … then tomatoes like the rain!' 'Like the rain?' 'Like it's raining tomatoes! An Italian taught me. For tomatoes, Tondo Roma and San Marzano are the best ones, verdad, my little wop? But anyway haz lo que quieras, mon ami, do whatever the fuck you want. That's my own ragù alla napoletana, e vaffanculo. Others do de otra manera, I don't give a shit.'

I listened, marvelling at his knowledge and at his gold teeth, which I glimpsed from time to time when he coughed or when he paused mid-sentence with his mouth open. He'd often get stuck on Italian or Spanish and fill the gap with French or Portuguese: 'The police, you know … les flics hablan only one tongue … tongue, idioma, lengua, como se dice … old sea dog like me habla toutes les langues … ' Then he'd continue, in tentative English: 'Italian immigrants came to Britannia before it was cool, in the sixties, before the Beatles … then they put restaurants and shops in London and Edinburgh, barber shops. Muy bueno haircut chez les wops! Anyway, just a few sailors, todos shopkeepers or constructors … como se dice … builders! So, in London Italians can't find involtini meat like the butchers in Naples, mamma mia! So they make pasta sauce with mince meat, like they do in Bologna. So they call it Bolognaise, capeesh, mon ami?'

What I gleaned from Silver's words was that all these Neapolitans who came to the UK started making pasta sauce using a recipe from northern Italy instead, because it was easier to find lard and minced meat than olive oil and whole chunks of meat: the Bolognaise mystery had thus been solved. Quite why, however, pizza with spicy salami ended up being called 'pepperoni' ('peppers' in Italian) is still beyond me — and on this point, not even John Silver could provide any clarification.

After this pleasant digression through culinary history, it's time to introduce the apprentice the boss assigned to me one day. Rodrigo came from South America, and as such he was generally lumped in with the so-called 'PIGS' alongside his Mediterranean cousins from Portugal, Italy, Greece, and Spain. We made a wonderful couple: me, an iconoclastic romantic, an astute brute who disdained all and sundry; and Rodrigo, an eighteen-year-old streetwise pizza ferret from Ecuador, a remarkable specimen from a fast-paced breed, who went about his life in a blur of hectic activity. Silver called him 'el mozo' ('the cabin boy') — half-waiter, half-errand boy, he was a jack-of-all-trades and master of none.

Fast by nature, he appeared diligent and hard-working, but it was all a front. He was forever buzzing to and fro, yet achieving fuck all in the process. As much as he enjoyed setting new speed records as the bosses looked on in utter amazement, perhaps only one out of his 700 frenzied movements per second resulted in actual work getting done; for the most part, his activities consisted of smiling at female customers, scratching his groin, spitting in the flour, shoving me, and humping the kitchen counter, with a couple of push-ups and salsa steps thrown in for good measure. His elaborate performance was expertly disguised as labour, so much so that at first he had me fooled too, and I thought he was a real workhorse. But he cheated like a pro, at the speed of light. He was like a revved-up engine with the gear stick permanently stuck in neutral. All that senseless toiling irritated me. And Rodrigo seemed to say: 'Hey chico, the fuck you doing, man? *Cálmate* — take it easy. We can cheat together and fuck the boss, hey?'

And cheat we did. Rodrigo cheated outrageously and Silver eagerly joined in, enthusiasm making the ex-junkie veins on his forearms pop: 'Carajo — a la mierda la fucking boss madam. We put up a fucking bluff, mes amis!' At times, Rodrigo's game reached such vertiginous, metaphysical heights that he openly mocked the bosses by calling his own bluff: he thoroughly enjoyed showing them that it was all bluster, that they were deluding themselves if they thought he was going to let them exploit him for a few pieces of tin emblazoned with the Queen's profile.

Once, for instance, we hadn't finished preparing the pizza toppings and the restaurant was due to open in half an hour, so Rodrigo — proud and stiff like a Soviet apparatchik who'd just overseen a successful five-year plan — announced to the boss that the pizza chefs wouldn't be eating that day, because there was too much to do. Besides, there was no one manning the main kitchen: Silver had vanished without a trace. The pantry pirate suddenly reappeared, his eyelids even droopier than usual.

'Vuelvo de lo fucking chopin …' he said, slurring his words.

'Chopin as in the famous composer?'

'No — choping, to buy, comprar, capeesh?'

Shopping! 'Sì, fucking chopin en el supermercado. Now I put the stuff in the freezer and we start, dále cabrón! And we work hasta la muerte, until we drop!'

Deeply moved by our dedication, the *signora* gestured to everyone else to sit and eat while we got down to work in the kitchen. After five minutes, however, we sat down too — 'But only for a quick bite!' we scrupulously informed the boss. Silver, sly sailor that he was, promised, in his Spanglish: 'Today we work like mad dogs aquí en la kitchen! No time, only comida rapida, eat fast! Fucking hell!'

After another five minutes everyone got up except the pizza chefs — that is, myself and Rodrigo (Silver, for his part, rarely ate anything but opiates). Five hundred 'quick bites' and fifty minutes later, Rodrigo and I were still lounging at the table under the boss's livid gaze: precarious piles of scampi tails littered our plates, and the unmanned pizza counter was in a right state. 'So much for a quick bite!' said the *signora*, 'I don't even know if you're lazy or just plain stupid anymore!' It was our way of taking the piss: we'd build up the bosses' expectations and then leave them in the lurch.

At other times we kept our own counsel, like a couple of wizened gunslingers who didn't even need to take aim to shoot the enemy down — and like all self-respecting gunslingers, we watched our backs, ready to snarl at the *signora* if we caught her giving us disapproving looks. Rodrigo was the kind of guy who would dart inside the oven to turn a pizza, then climb back out and roll another three at the speed of light, all while sneezing audibly in order to fake an improbable allergy to flour. He was possessed: one second he'd be tossing a chunk of tuna on a piece of focaccia that was already burning (shit!), the next he'd be literally running circles around me, lining up plates, frothing at the mouth and swearing like a trucker after banging his head against the marble kitchen counter.

Sometimes, Silver would come and help us out ('Dále, c'mon, son of a bitch! La puta madre que te parió ... ') and Rodrigo's fake sneezes would get louder and louder (aaachoooo!) as he waved at his Ecuadorean friends waiting outside the restaurant. At the end of the day, he'd clean up faster than an F1 mechanic pumping up tyres at a pit stop, sing a few lines from an Ecuadorian cumbia song ('no trates de cansarme, yo, yo no me canso'), blow away the flour from the counter, hop on a scooter, and vanish into the night like a ghost.

That was Rodrigo for you: like a pixie he'd jump into the oven, bounce off a shelf, and re-emerge from a sack of flour all white and powdery like the bosom of a Versailles courtesan, then guzzle straight from the beer pump while the waitresses slogged away and the oven vault cracked and the pizzas burned.

Rodrigo fantasised about girls so hot our oven would get jealous. Girls that would fire up our tired pizza chef-hearts. In his dreams, Rodrigo and I would make love with all those girls — girls we drew with our finger on the floury counter, girls we imagined or saw or made up or ripped out from *The Sun*'s page 3. In those dreams there was no room for the pizza orders the waitresses tore from their notebooks and pinned on the board, because the waitresses themselves would be joining the ecstatic orgies, our bodies cavorting on the sacks of Premiato Mulino Molinari Enrico flour: doggy style on the 30lb sacks, cowgirl on the 50lb ones, missionary on the double-zero flour bags, and — in the crowning moment of our lascivious debauchery — the whole front of house staff would pile up atop the ten sacks of organic Manitoba flour, in scenes of such depravity that they would make Hogarth's 'Gin Lane' appear a paragon of piety.

These were the fantasies us poor pantry pirates indulged in: our impure hearts forever on a sacred quest for the fabled treasure calzone, stuffed with gold. This is who we were.

And now let us move on to yet another little ploy we'd devised to take revenge on our oppressors. For the customers, as you can imagine, a few drops of laxative would suffice: an age-old remedy against arrogance and insolence that puts the fear of God into every pompous consumer of refined carbs. With the *signora*, it was more complicated. As much as we were tempted to throw the capitalist pig in the bin and walk away whistling 'The Red Flag', we couldn't afford such drastic measures. The plan we came up with was much subtler and really quite elaborate: we would make her stick her head in the kitchen bin.

As it happened, the *signora* had a habit of hovering around the pizza oven all day, ostensibly to inspect god knows what paperwork, but in reality going cross-eyed from the effort of monitoring our every movement. Her ears were also finely tuned to our conversations, which she eagerly scanned for evidence that we were talking about her behind her back. And so — spiteful and ungrateful employees that we were — every time a waitress showed up, out of breath, carrying plates full of leftovers, we'd whisper, loudly enough for her to hear: 'Oh, they sent a pizza back!' When a customer sent a pizza back, it was usually because it was burnt, or too bland, or the toppings were wrong.

Anyway, 'pizza back' was the magic phrase: the *signora*, who up until that point had feigned indifference, would scuttle into the kitchen and plunge head-first into the bin, leaving the cash register at the mercy of our light-fingered chef. After furiously rummaging through the rubbish, she'd re-emerge with arms lathered in coleslaw, chicken bones lodged in her rolled-up sleeves, rice stuck under her fingernails and hands reeking of tuna — but no trace of the discarded pizza. She'd keep wading through that bog, covered in gunk, and still the offending pizza would elude her. At times, a few pizzas would indeed find their way to the bin, but on those occasions we'd obviously keep it to ourselves, and at any rate the waitresses always took care to bury them under an avalanche of mussel shells. But when, alas, she did unearth a pizza that had actually been sent back, there was no stopping her: she'd stand there stern-faced and give us a good talking-to.

She wanted us to confess our sins in full, to repent and beg for forgiveness: we were summoned to the kitchen bin as if to the confessional booth. Brandishing the offending item, she would analyse the reasons it was sent back — it was overcooked, or undercooked, or what have you. And if we dared point out that it was, in fact, cooked just right, undeterred by our objections she'd bite off a chunk and swallow it together with a lipstick-encrusted cigarette end: 'See? Tastes awful!' (no shit, it probably tastes of Rouge Coco No. 5 and nicotine on a bed of burnt flour). And the productive, lucrative penance she'd demand to atone for our mortal sins consisted of fifty pizzas to be rolled, seasoned, and cooked free of charge — in the name of the Father, the Son, and the Holy Ghost.

This, in short, was the dehumanising life we led in the restaurant. It was only natural that, in order to survive, I'd jump at every opportunity to stage a mutiny. At the slightest provocation from the *signora* or her husband, I'd stir up discontent and foment all kinds of rebellion. There were times when tensions seemed to reach boiling point, but whether it was inertia or the fear of losing a safe bed in the dorm above the restaurant, sooner or later we patched things up.

Speaking of beds, we shared our spacious mansion with Silver, much to our chagrin seeing as his old carcass bounced up and down on the mattress all night, ravaged by an incessant cough. The old sailor was forever coughing. His lungs were done in, wrecked after a life spent toiling from port to port: he'd worked on cargo ships in the merchant navy and insulated the holds of an entire container fleet. He'd breathed in all manner of toxic substances and aromatic hydrocarbons, and on top of that he still smoked. As a result, as soon as he lay down on his bed he'd start coughing and couldn't fall asleep: he had to take a powerful sedative to send him into the arms of Morpheus.

One day, when I was all bunged up with a terrible cold, Silver gifted me a little bottle of concentrated codeine solution — fifteen drops and I was out like a light. Afterwards, I continued taking a few drops every night before bed, even though the cold was gone. Those of you who have worked the late shift in a restaurant will know what I'm talking about: it's hard to fall asleep when the tinny sound of cutlery and cups jumbled up in the sink or the dishwasher follows you all the way to your bed. A few drops of that stuff and I'd drift off into a peaceful sleep, although it would sometimes give me heartburn or nausea in the morning.

It was precisely during one such rude awakening that we had an idea. We knew that the reputation of many restaurants hinges on the silence of loyal staff who witness all sorts of grubby and unsavoury practices in the kitchen. Well, fed up with keeping quiet, one day we started 'Operation Unsealed Lips': when we weren't made to slave away in the kitchen, we'd take it upon ourselves to spread embarrassing rumours about our restaurant in that area of Bristol. In other words, we had come up with our very own form of non-violent (for once) protest for the hospitality sector. Rodrigo, Silver, and I, aka the Dream Team, divvied up the area between the three of us and walked the streets day and night preaching our unholy Gospel in broken English.

Silver took the lead — and thank fuck for that, because his English was better than mine (which wasn't saying much, really). I ventured a few tentative phrases myself, such as 'fucking food delivery' and 'you shit what you eat, you eat what you shit', which, as usual, mostly generated confusion. Like the personification of Fame herself — according to the poet Virgil, a swift, birdlike monster with as many eyes, lips, tongues, and ears as feathers, spreading real and fake news alike — I walked for miles, from one Italian restaurant to the next, shouting profanities and spreading stories that were well received by our competitors.

'Do we have a fish menu? You bet we do — we offer a delicious seafood soup, a special recipe of our chef Long John Silver's, made from leftover lobsters from the day before: we scrape up all the meat residue from the shells, then chuck it in the food processor, strain the mixture through a sieve and add ketchup to dye it red. A true delicacy! You prefer meat, you say? Then why not try our legendary brisket aux trois vins: we marinate a generic cut of tough meat in vinegar, then mask the taste with Silver's trademark, ultra-spicy "Buccaneer's sauce"! Would you like to know what goes in the sauce? No? Not interested? Ah well, goodbye then … come visit us soon!'

If every day had been like that, life wouldn't have been so bad. I mean, I'd take any excuse to run riot with Rodrigo and Silver, sure — but the place was slowly sapping my will to live. And on top of that I hadn't learnt a single word of English: what the hell had I come to Bristol for?

My suffering reached its peak at mealtimes — the worst time of the day as far as I was concerned. Our Italian bosses considered eating with the staff a sacred duty, a holy communion with their employees. And like all solemn celebrations, it came with a sermon. The husband would start by reminding us that the world was full of thieves and Muslims and slackers, all of whom deserved to be shot. And the *signora* egged him on, like a public prosecutor in court. Then there were the gays, who were sick, and wouldn't they just die already instead of going around spitting in glasses and spreading AIDS and whatnot. And let's not forget junkies and thugs and immigrants (except those who worked in our restaurant, of course): they too deserved to be shot.

At this point, everyone looked at Silver to see if he had anything to say on the matter — because you see, my dear readers, some of the old sea dog's former associates were, as they say, 'known to the police' for misdemeanours ranging from cattle rustling and smuggling to illegal fishing of protected species. Not to mention his history of substance abuse: as much as he swore those days were behind him, he seemed to know the active ingredients of every prescription drug under the sun and could even cook them up following his own bespoke recipes. Silver, then, would eat quickly and say to me: 'Vamonos, little wop, time to learn mas knots.' The atmosphere, in short, was not exactly pleasant, and the bosses looked at us disapprovingly, suspecting we didn't entirely agree with them.

Weekends were even worse, because Edward, the bosses' son — their pride and joy and most prized possession — would take a break from his prestigious university studies to join us for lunch and dinner. During said meals he'd proudly announce that he was a teetotaller (and that alcoholics should be lobotomised); that he was a virgin (and that those who had sex should be arrested); that he didn't smoke, that he respected speed limits, never ran a red light, never forgot to pay vehicle tax for his moped, always flushed the toilet, never jumped a queue, he didn't even drip coming out of the shower — you get the picture. As for those who fell foul of these rules ... well, by his standards, Rodrigo, Silver, and I should all be sent to the gallows.

I really couldn't stand him. He triggered in me the same feverish impatience with which I tore dried clumps of dough off of my forearms before going to bed. The problem, of course, was that the bosses had the upper hand — and they harassed me. I didn't clean up thoroughly enough, I left a pernicious trail of flour in my wake wherever I went, I was forever letting hard-boiled eggs go off in the tubs — which happened several times, making me a repeat offender and upgrading my charge sheet from involuntary to gross negligence.

Furthermore, during the preliminary hearings, the boss established I was being aided and abetted by Silver and Rodrigo, which implied a conspiracy and constituted a further aggravating factor. Rumour had it that my heinous crimes were even premeditated. These, in increasing order of ferocity, were the barbaric atrocities I stood accused of: spilling brine from the caper jar in the fridge, jamming the mozzarella grinder, letting anchovies go off in the tubs — villainy and knavery the likes of which had never been seen before!

I was also suspected of engaging in illicit relationships between Roman Catholics and members of the Church of England. This called for an exemplary punishment — perhaps even capital punishment, as my good friend Edward strongly advocated. But the *signora* — ever the pragmatist — considered capital punishment inefficient, not reforming, and ultimately unprofitable; my sentence was therefore commuted to forced labour, along with solitary confinement and sensory deprivation during non-working hours — necessary, in her eyes, to curb my morbid interest in English waitresses.

The atmosphere was, in short, intolerably oppressive for us pizza chefs, and I had proof that my locker was being routinely searched for evidence of my wrongdoing. I remember losing my temper one day, shouting and kicking furniture in the dining room. It was in response to the umpteenth punitive task the *signora*, clearly motivated by her hatred for the British waitresses, had imposed on the girls: after an excruciating shift, she'd ordered them to scrub the legs of all the tables and chairs. It was through such measures that she aimed to punish the guilty, encourage the righteous, and warn off the evil-minded — predictably, however, this only earned her more insults and abuse.

It couldn't last, and it didn't. One day I made a strange discovery in the girls' changing room; something inside me cracked, and the crack kept getting wider and wider. It happened like this: the boss had temporarily stored some of the larger tomato tins in that room, and the *signora* kicked up a fuss, shouting they were to be immediately taken down to the basement where they belonged. Seeing as that room was close to the kitchen, I thought I'd better grab a few tins while I could, so I wouldn't have to haul them up from the basement.

Stepping into that room for the first time, my nostrils were assailed by a foul smell of rotten fish. The lightbulb had blown and I couldn't see a thing, so I went and rummaged for a torch in one of the kitchen drawers. I thought something had died and was rotting away in there, and I decided to hunt it out. Following my nose, I moved a sofa and a heavy curtain out of the way, and eventually glimpsed a tiny nook in the wall, hidden from prying eyes. I pressed on, undeterred by the disheartening stench, and aimed the torch at the nook.

The blood froze in my veins. In the alcove was what looked like a small doll. The head was that of a tentacled sea creature — an octopus maybe, or a squid — jet-black, it gleamed like volcanic glass. A macabre wig had been arranged on top of the idol's head: a kind of powdery, strawberry-blonde wig in a puffy eighties' hairdo. Whatever the hell it was, it was utterly disturbing.

Suddenly, my heart was racing and my ears were pounding. Vertigo. Tension. Anxiety. Jabbing pain in my guts. Cold sweats. Goosebumps. My mouth was dry and my clothes stuck to my clammy skin. I stepped back, catching my breath, then bolted out of the cursed room.

Back in the dining room, customers were eating peacefully as always, their voices a reassuring hum punctuated only by the clinking of cutlery and the waitresses shouting orders in the kitchen. I got back to work, haunted by the memory of the voodoo doll.

—

That night, tormented by the image of the bizarre idol, I couldn't sleep. I reached for Silver's sedative and upped the dose. The drops tasted weird, bitter with a sweet aftertaste. Citrus, honey, cocoa perhaps, thyme, caramel: synthetic flavours to mask the taste of the potent opioids. Twenty-five drops in a splash of water. My thoughts drifted away as an obscure force pulled me down into oblivion.

The following morning I felt nauseous. When I approached the coffee pot my stomach mutinied: that horrific vision materialised before my eyes. Determined to put an end to my paranoia, I resolved to get to the bottom of the mystery. I went downstairs and found the kitchen still empty. I sneaked into the sinister room with the same apprehension I had felt as a child when my grandmother told me the Bogeyman would take me away if I didn't behave. Said Bogeyman was a dastardly-looking wooden figurine purchased at the flea market, which she placed by my bedroom door to prevent me from getting up during the enforced afternoon siesta. After baking a cake in her wood-fired range, she'd promptly hide it in the kitchen cupboard, guarded by that same Bogeyman. She knew I had a sweet tooth and I'd try to steal some, so — like the seasoned farmer that she was — she resorted to the tried-and-tested scarecrow method. Nothing terrified me like that bastard wooden figurine.

I shifted the sofa again, aimed the torch at the nook and

… nothing. There was nothing there. Absolutely fuck all. I began to think I'd been had — what if the *signora*, like my gran, used the blond-wigged fetish to keep the staff away from the restaurant safe, the treasure chest John Silver had spent months poking around searching for? You'd often see him shifting furniture, lifting paintings or tapping on the walls. Maybe the *signora* had sussed out his plan and was trying to scare us with this charade. But in that case, why had she tidied it away already? Had the idol ever really been there?

Paradoxically, seeing perfectly smooth white plaster where I'd expected to find the figurine disturbed me even more. I went back to work and never found the uncanny shrine again.

And yet I had seen it with my own two eyes. I was certain of it.

Although I steered well clear of it I was somehow drawn to the little room. I sensed a kind of negative energy radiating from it, draining the staff's morale and sapping their intellect. Little accidents kept happening every day. The waitresses seemed to be wasting away — black circles formed around their eyes, one stumbled and broke a rib, another busted a vein in her leg. And despite the ventilation system, the place smelt like a sewer: the stench of rotten fish followed me around everywhere, and the idol came to me in my dreams. Who was behind the sinister statuette? Why did they keep it hidden in an alcove? And where had it gone? I didn't dare talk about it with anyone. I kept working. One minute I'd hobble like Silver, the next I'd be darting around the place like Rodrigo, although his energy, too, appeared diminished now. In the grip of paranoia, I almost felt responsible for what was happening to my colleagues. Had I inadvertently opened Pandora's box — or nook — and unleashed an evil curse on the restaurant? And what, exactly, was the *signora*'s role in all this? I remembered hearing her bragging about being able to get rid of the evil eye. Once, I'd glimpsed her through the door of the little room, intently smearing the waitresses' foreheads with olive oil from a plate with a red chilli balanced on the rim.

Those were dark days indeed; my heart swelled with anger, and yet I felt completely apathetic. Desperate, my skin salty with encrusted sweat, I took out my frustration on the innocent sacks of flour. And still I kept going, day in day out, spitting in the oven, the image of the idol etched in my memory as my saliva sizzled away among the pizzas, exhaling foul vapours of horror. Onwards, *adelante, avanti.*

That is the question

I was told immediately that 'they' would never allow it. Who were 'they'? I asked. Nobody seemed to know; but evidently 'they' were omnipotent.

George Orwell, *The Road to Wigan Pier*

And now let us take a step back. Pisa airport. Check-in desk. The place was crawling with suits. I could feel my parents' eyes firmly anchored on the back of my head as I lifted the ugly blue plastic bag onto the scales, with some effort. That was odd. Renato, my dad, had insisted on carrying the bag himself, and it didn't seem that heavy: the last time I'd picked it up, the handles didn't cut into my hands.

The lady at the desk looked at me in utter amazement: the bag was three times over the weight limit and I didn't know what to do. They explained I had to take a few items out … most items, to be precise. I unzipped the bag and at that point Renato butted in: unbeknown to me, it transpired, he'd slipped in a plumber's spanner and a 3 kg pipe wrench, as well as his beloved farrier rasp and other assorted tools. My mum Francesca, for her part, had contributed an iron. Nice one, Ma.

However, when I began removing the rasp and a hammer,

all hell broke loose. Renato grabbed the discarded tools and brandished them ominously, shouting profanities to the British Airways flight assistants who, meanwhile, had gathered around us to enjoy the show: 'The fuck you looking at? Go back to Pisa!' (You should know, my dear readers, that for anyone born in Livorno — or indeed in Florence — hailing from neighbouring Pisa is the worst imaginable insult. Dante himself, in his immense wisdom, went as far as wishing that the river Arno would flood the town and drown all its inhabitants.)

Things escalated quickly and Renato started yelling at me like it was all my fault: 'No one wants tools anymore, hey? Too posh for a spanner? Afraid to get your hands dirty or what?' Then to the airline crew: 'Do you think the hammer is for Prince Charles? God forbid! The screwdriver and spanner are for my son!' I held him back, fearing he'd start hammering the check-in desk. 'We're off to a good start,' I thought.

I knew I should have asked them not to come to the airport — in their eyes, I was leaving for good. But they were only trying to help, my parents; they only wanted to make sure I had the tools I needed to survive away from home — you never know when a spanner might come in handy. They hadn't realised things had moved on: the economy had been 'dematerialised' and manual labour was a thing of the past (or so they said). Anyway, in the end they called security and my dad was escorted out of the departures area. Unfazed, he lit a cigarette and struck up a conversation with one of the guards.

Back at the check-in desk, I was begrudgingly handed a boarding pass and instructed to make my way through security.

First, however, I had to say goodbye to Francesca, who was already in tears. Through the glass walls I could see Renato gesticulating — probably trying to unionise the luggage carriers. I joined him outside, and as soon as he saw me he resumed his sermon: 'See, son? No one wants tools anymore. Can't travel to England with a hammer and a spanner, turns out. Just as well spanners were invented in England, so they'll sell them in London too I reckon, won't they?'

'Just as well,' I replied.

He pressed on: 'See the way they put on airs, these little people with their little ties, and for what? For weighing other people's luggage? Come off it. They're afraid of real work, hey?' He was smiling now.

'Dad, I've got to go …'

'All right, son … now, from the plane you'll get a good look at this famous tower of Pisa … can't even trust them to run a proper building site, these dimwits. It came out all lopsided their tower … you go tell the English that! And say hello to the Queen for me … wish I was minted like her!' He joked to mask his discomfort. He'd never been on a plane.

'Right, off with you then,' he continued, 'you'll never know …'

'You'll never know if you don't try,' I echoed. Reassured by this universal truth and by a paternal pat on the back, I went through the security checks, and — for the first time in my life — stepped onto a plane.

It wasn't just my dad's tools weighing me down in the departures lounge, but the assorted failures and emotional baggage I carried with me everywhere. I was a provincial peasant who'd never seen the world. Once a promising full-back in the local football youth division and scion of one of Tuscany's finest working-class families, I had turned my back on both and bet all my money on the wrong horse: a degree. I had forged myself a pair of intellectual wax wings which — predictably — had melted when I dared fly too close to the sun that kisses the rich.

I should have listened to my father — he had it all figured out. The working-class education system was an unstoppable production line conveying youngsters from the local youth division through to a vocational qualification in technology or manufacturing, and then straight into the Piombino steelworks and a life of *catenaccio* tactics in one of the many working men's football clubs.

'The boy's strong, but has he got the drive?' 'There's talent there, but he needs practice.' How many times had I heard these comments from the old guard? 'If he's really good he could make it into the *Eccellenza* league … maybe even *Serie D*.' That was the brilliant future I could aspire to at the age of twelve: cutting my teeth on the muddy football pitches of the youth league, learning the ropes, 'growing a spine' as they used to say, like John Wayne with his black eyepatch. And then — triumphant like Tardelli after scoring the decisive goal in the 1982 World Cup final against Germany — walking through the steelworks turnstile in my native Piombino. A whole life in the shadow of those blast furnaces.

I, however, foolishly thought paper could cut scissors, and bet everything on books. The odds of a factory worker's son surviving outside his natural habitat are about thirty-five to one — but I was stubborn, and anxious to explore the uncharted waters beyond the steel plant stacks. So little by little, one step at a time, I walked away from that plant.

It helped that, at school, everything came easy to me. I didn't even have to try. I just knew the stuff without even studying. Concepts seemed to flow effortlessly through my brain like oil through an engine, without foaming, clearing soot from cylinders and pistons. Ideas poured out of me and neatly arranged themselves onto pages, smooth like the varnish carpenters apply to wood after sanding it — no lumps, no dripping.

To be clear, it's not like I was some sort of child prodigy. Quite simply, I was encouraged to learn. My town was home to a collective of rebel Jesuits who, in the seventies, had founded an after-school club in our working-class neighbourhood, and even an experimental school. By the eighties most of the Jesuits had left, but the educators, who had been trained on Freire's seminal *Pedagogy of the Oppressed*, remained. They'd send us out to conduct neighbourhood surveys after school and encourage us to print our own little magazine. From a very early age they inspired us to demand curiosity and honesty from our schoolteachers. They told us it would help us become 'key players in global history'. They told us that when someone asked us what we wanted to be when we grew up, we shouldn't answer 'engineer' or 'architect', but: 'when I grow up I want to change the world'.

To be honest, all we really cared about was not being ripped off by the rich — that is, the friends and associates of this mythical creature our dads referred to as 'the Man': he'd never been sighted around the neighbourhood, but no one doubted his existence. So we had to keep our wits about us and never let an injustice go unpunished. Or, as our dads were very fond of saying: if life gives you lemons, you chuck 'em right back at life.

But as our afterschool educators would say, we're talking about different kinds of lemons here: you need to use your head. And use our heads we did — mostly, at first, to headbutt our enemies. The Jesuits patiently wiped the blood from our faces, explaining to us that there were such things as metaphors. And so, metaphor by metaphor, in the end we stopped smashing heads and started reading, studying, and investigating in our own impulsive, hot-tempered way.

If Renato never stood in the way of my passion for books and metaphors, Francesca, my mum, was positively enthusiastic about it. Dad wasn't big on books but religiously bought his newspaper — which he consumed in full, starting from the sports pages — every day. Mum, meanwhile, was a rather omnivorous reader, and she gladly indulged my love of literature. As a result, no one at home was surprised when my teachers began saying that I was 'academically gifted', although I had never actually been seen to do my homework.

'Always with his nose stuck in a book, this one.' And to be fair, my mum's nose was also regularly stuck in a book, so the apple didn't fall far from the tree. As I grew up, my teachers kept praising my 'natural disposition to study', my 'photographic memory', and 'concise style', although they also said 'at times we do catch him plagiarising'. That stung. I stopped plagiarising and started playing tricks with words: I carried my thesaurus to school and systematically swapped regular terms with obscure synonyms whose actual meaning I often ignored.

This tendency to 'inflate' sentences was rooted in the naïve belief that important people used difficult words, and that it was all these difficult words that made them so importantly incomprehensible to us commoners. As a result, my essays became unreadable and completely meaningless. My teacher explained to me that the real trick was using simple words to describe complex things. I changed tack and started imitating the style of the authors I read, which was a lot more fun. I devoured books, especially Dumas and Stevenson, but also science fiction, reading almost every single thing Asimov wrote. My essays were teeming with musketeers and robots and pirates, and my mum would come back beaming from parent-teacher evenings because she'd been told 'how well he writes, Madam! And such a prodigious imagination!'

But it wasn't simply imagination — I was hungry, properly hungry. It was more like book binging, a physical urge to consume pages, instigated and fuelled by the rebel Jesuits. It was the ancestral, primeval hunger of generations of the dispossessed who had been denied access to culture. In my early teens I was, in short, voracious. Insatiable. Other kids read, I attacked books: I bit and chewed and metabolised them into tools, my very own workshop made of metaphors and ideas, just like my dad's workshop in the basement.

My teachers said it would be a pity if I chose a vocational qualification over the *liceo* — the secondary schools that prepare you for university in Italy. 'Do tell your mum, will you?' 'Tell her what?' 'That you really should be going to a *liceo*.' So I did tell her — but not my dad, not straight away. I wasn't sure how it would go down. Reading books was all fine and dandy, but studying to go to university was a different matter altogether. Mind you, he went back to school too, in a way — spurred by their union, he and his colleagues signed up to the scheme offering 150 paid hours to each employee to further their education, and Renato decided he was going to get a vocational qualification. He started one of those correspondence courses for factory workers — a bit like the electronics diploma offered by Scuola Radio Elettra that was very popular in Italy in those years.

After a while, however, he couldn't be bothered anymore, especially when it came to writing essays — writing really wasn't his thing. 'I'll write your essays, Dad!' I'd say. But my mum shushed me: 'Can't you see your father's knackered — he picks up a book and falls asleep, bless him, because he's been away working for ten days straight, all so you and your sister can go to school without a care in the world.' When Dad came back from his long shifts in the refineries of northern Italy, he always carried a big duffel bag full of overalls covered in a peculiar fine grey dust.

Meanwhile, Renato had begun my initiation into factory life. On those rare rainy weekends when he couldn't take me to a local football match, he'd started teaching me the rudiments of mechanics. I didn't know how to tell him about the whole *liceo* thing, but one day, unexpectedly, he brought it up himself.

We were driving on the Strada Statale Aurelia and trying to catch the latest football scores on the radio. Suddenly he turned down the volume, and in a serious tone asked me what I wanted to be when I grow up. 'Footballer,' I replied. 'I mean for real,' he retorted. 'Welder,' I replied. Pause. 'After the *liceo*, that is.'

'Yes, your mum told me. You want to study science and maths, right?'

'It wasn't my idea,' I continued. 'Mum wants me to go. And my Italian literature teacher. And my history teacher. They say I might as well take classical literature.'

'Classical literature my arse,' he mumbled to himself, but loud enough for me to hear. 'If you do go, and take maths and science —' (the choice was already made) '— then you have to go to university. You sure you're up to it, son? No one in our family's ever gone to university.'

I said nothing, then resumed my manoeuvrings:

'But if I took classical literature ...'

'Classical literature is out of the question,' he cut me off.

That threw me. I felt bad, like I was asking for an expensive toy. Too expensive.

'Anyway I'm not going. I want to be a welder. Honest. I'll get a diploma in chemistry, or metallurgy. Or maybe mechanics. I'm not sure yet.'

'There's time,' he said, 'now put the radio back on will you? Check the scores on our betting slip.'

Volume up. 'Ah, here's Ameri again ... sorry, mate!' he said, apologising to the sports announcer.

After a couple of weeks he got back from another shift in the refineries up north, between the Vercelli rice paddies and the Ligurian Alps.

'Come and watch the footie with your Pa!'

I smiled. I liked watching football with my Pa. This 'Pa' thing is weird — where I come from, dad is *babbo*. 'Papa' is more common elsewhere in Italy, but in Tuscany only posh people use it. 'Pa' however, and 'Ma', are allowed — and I always thought that if my dad used it, it must be some old vernacular term from Livorno. Instead, it turns out he probably borrowed it from the Ligurian dialect — but I only learnt that long after he was gone. It was one of the many hybrid linguistic expressions that Renato, an itinerant welder, often used. Our family lexicon was made up of dozens of little affectionate terms and assorted profanities that he extracted from their geographical context, melted like scrap metal in the blast furnace that was his chest, and then forged on his lips.

'Listen to your Pa.'

'Yes, Dad.'

'What do you want to do next year.'

It wasn't a question. It was a statement, like an agenda item of a union meeting — and specifically, one taking place between father and son in the old Audi 80, once again on the Aurelia, once again listening to the football on the radio as we drove back home from Rosignano Solvay, full to bursting with Grandma's delicious liver crostini.

I was determined not to come across as one of those snobs who wanted to be architects or lawyers. A neighbour had suggested an alternative option: 'If you want to keep studying, why don't you go to the navy academy in Livorno? It's free and you'll get a good qualification. Some of their graduates even go to uni!'

I didn't know what this academy was, but it sounded like a sensible thing to do to save my parents some money. It's free, so why not? Navy academy it is, I thought.

We were down to the final couple of miles on the Aurelia: the strip of tarmac where, traditionally, we talked about personal stuff. It was here that my dad told me about that time he obliterated Grandpa's bike — which was also the only time the old man gave him a good whipping — or about Grandpa's heroic ploy to avoid being sent to the front during World War II. A farm labourer and bricklayer, he'd been inexplicably drafted into the cavalry regiment — so one day he jumped on the saddle, closed his eyes and let himself fall like a sack of potatoes off the horse's back, right onto a bramble thicket. He said the animal had bucked him off. They picked him up — with broken bones and riddled with thorns — and packed him off to the hospital, far from the front and from Mussolini's army. He didn't exactly have an easy time of it, but nothing compared to one of his friends who, to avoid being drafted, had pulled out his own teeth.

Every time we drove down that stretch of the Aurelia I thought of Grandpa Santi and his toothless friend. That day, however, my reverie was cut short by a question that wasn't a question. There was a hint of anxiety in my father's voice:

'So. About this school thing, then.'

I repeated what my neighbour told me the day before.

Then:

'I want to go to the navy academy in Livorno.'

To Renato, that was like a sucker-punch from the then middleweight champion, Marvelous Marvin Hagler. He was white as a sheet. He said nothing. Did nothing. For about 300 yards. Then all of a sudden he indicated, swerved, and slammed on the brakes, pulling over onto the hard shoulder. The car skidded in between two old plane trees — they're gone too now, chopped down years ago — we were practically in a ditch.

He leant over and grabbed me by the collar, pulling me close.

'Now listen here — you wanted to go to the Jesuits' afterschool club, you said it was because of a girl and I bought it. Now the navy academy — you expect me to believe you're chasing skirts there too? Have you gone mad or what? Have you lost your mind? What's in that big head of yours, hey? Don't you know they brainwash you in there? Are you stupid or what? Don't forget — I made you, and like I made you I'll break you — do you hear me? Navy academy my arse ... now you go straight to the *liceo* and study maths and science, you prick! And knuckle down, you twat ... and then off to university or I'll kick you in the teeth, I swear I will. Off to school with your tail between your legs — do you hear me? And when you're done studying, you better come and help out at the plant — not like that useless engineer of ours who never shows up and I have to do all the calculations myself off the top of my head, for Chrissakes!'

Rant over.

I could see I'd won.

'And remember,' he continued, 'you can study all you want, the important thing is to stick to The Rules.'

'What rules, Dad?'

'The ten commandments me and my colleagues have always lived by. Don't think that because you've got a degree you're going to brown-nose some toffs and be all pally-pals with them. Don't think you can shit on our commandments and get away with it.'

'What commandments?' I asked.

'Rules that apply in all plants and building sites, even abroad, for welders and for builders and everyone else. Simple rules: Help your mates. Strike. Don't be a brown-noser. Never cross a picket line. If you've got to fight, don't hit 'em too hard. And don't be too hard on those poor sods from Pisa …'

'They're people too, like us.'

'Well, son, they're animals too, like us.'

'Anything else?'

'Never trust a toff. If a toff calls you sir, stick your arse to the wall …'

'What?'

'Because when they speak like that it means they're about to fuck you over. So stick your arse to the wall and don't bloody let them! Anyway, there's a couple more I can't remember now, but they're universal rules that apply everywhere in the world: a guy who'd gone to work on an offshore oil platform in Scotland told me they use them too. They're exactly the same — even in the North Sea. So watch it, son — and mind you toe the line. Study all you like but don't get cheeky — you're my son and you can't betray The Rules. If I catch you with a toff, I'll kick you in the teeth even on your graduation day. Now knuckle down.'

Message received. 'And what if I break a rule?'

'If you break my rules then I'll break something of yours … And I'll tell you one thing. There was this guy once, it's not like he was a scab or anything, he was just a tad too nice to the foreman, see what I mean? Like he'd bring him wine, cheese, eggs … and this created problems, at least in my team. So guess what I did to him.'

'You beat him up!'

'No need. At the end of the shift, he opened his locker and his clothes weren't there. Look up, I say to him. And there they were, nicely laid out on the ceiling. Nailed to the plasterboard. And his shoes too — riveted. All nice and ironed. He could have gone to a wedding in those clothes, I'm telling you.'

'Don't worry, Dad — you'll never catch me brown-nosing one of those toffs!'

'I hope so, son — I hope so. Wouldn't want to have to iron your clothes too.'

That conversation makes it sound like it was a spur-of-the moment kind of decision, whereas in fact my mum had been conducting lengthy diplomatic negotiations on my behalf for months, resulting in the rational, sensible conclusion reached by Renato. I wanted to go to a *liceo* and study literature, he wanted me to get a diploma in mechanics — in the end we reached a satisfactory compromise: I'd be going to a *liceo* but studying science and maths. None of this would have been possible without Francesca's support. She read everything — the good stuff and the bad stuff, high literature and romance novels, Cassola and Liala, Gadda and De Amicis. All her books would eventually find their way to me, and I'd get sucked right into the pages.

Sometimes we all read together — Francesca engrossed in Calvino, myself in Dumas, and my little sister Chiara in one of her colouring books. I remember those long winter weekends when it was too cold to play outside, Dad was away for work, and the Japanese cartoons on the few TV channels we had at the time wouldn't start until mid-afternoon. So we read. I started with comics and then moved on to the musketeers' saga. I was naïve enough to believe that, just as in those novels, injustice would not go unpunished in real life either: D'Artagnan would always swoop in and save the day on the last page.

As soon as I finished a book I had to start a new one. I loved going to the local bookshop. The owner had a prodigious memory: you just had to tell him which book you wanted and he'd dig it out from underneath stacks of volumes, shifting boxes and lifting shelves as he rooted around for it. And what he didn't have on the shelves he'd order from an enormous catalogue with tissue-thin pages that listed all the available titles. That tiny shop smelt of old presswork: Pirandello's plays, illustrated children's books — old editions that were all but out of print.

To me, that place wasn't a bookshop: it was a sanctuary. But I couldn't afford to buy much, so I'd go to the library — which, in keeping with the town's working-class heritage, was in the Palazzo del Forno Quadro, the site of Italy's very first blast furnace dating back to the sixteenth century: before my town even had a church, it had a foundry. The building now housed the town library, which in the eighties had hosted Europe's largest Trotskyist conference. During the long summer holidays I'd go to the library twice a day. At 9 am I'd go in, walk past an enormous blow-up of Trotsky in the hallway, and borrow a volume from the *Urania* sci-fi series. At 3 pm I'd go back, return the first book and borrow another. Two sci-fi novels a day: that was the extent of my summers, which I spent reading in my grandma's vegetable garden.

The librarian called me '*Signor Prunetti*'. 'You should read the great European authors, *Signor Prunetti*,' he said to me one day. Undeterred, I borrowed Asimov's *I, Robot*. He checked it out with a huge stamp — delivering a devastating blow that echoed for minutes and produced a swirling cloud of dust — then sneaked in a few more sci-fi titles from beyond the Iron Curtain. And an essay on the Molotov–Ribbentrop pact. And an account of Trotsky's Mexican exile. And a book on Jean Vigo's cinematography.

And so the days and the books went by, and a combination of my love of literature, my mother's support, and my father's utter contempt for the navy academy eventually landed me in a *liceo* rather than a vocational college. That, however, meant walking away from the steelworks, from the local football team, and — inevitably — from my childhood friends, who didn't want anything to do with me anymore. Which is to say they actively took the piss out of me.

'Prunetti's too good for us now — hey, smart arse?' 'What's the matter, Prunetti, don't you want to play with us anymore? Afraid you'll get your arse kicked or what?' Not even Pingone, the mechanic's son, wanted anything to do with me anymore. We'd been friends since he sat next to me in school one day in year 7. I liked him because he taught me how to do a wheelie on my bike. I enjoyed timing how long he could keep his front wheel off the ground, and if our bikes broke his brother would come out of the garage, with hands black as tar, and fix them. I will always remember him — he was a father figure of sorts for us, because he was repeating the year and consequently knew a great deal more than we did.

He'd started off with a bang on the first day of school. The school secretary had messed up and forgotten to update the class register, so his name was left out. The bell rang and the teacher came in — she was new and had only taught in posh schools before. 'Morning all,' she said. 'How are we today, how was your summer, bet you've all been somewhere nice …' and we all looked at her like: 'What the hell is she on about? We're lucky they didn't pack us off to work in some factory because it's against the law, but I still had to weed and water Grandpa's garden and watch the chickens and collect the eggs from the coop and if I broke one I'd get a right bollocking.' Then the smiling teacher, who had long wavy hair with a centre parting and wore a light wool jumper, proceeded to do a roll call. The polite ones (the geeks) stood up when they were called, the rest got away with a half-arsed upward motion. Anyway, after a string of here-here-here, she went: 'Lovely, we're all here.'

At that point the guy sitting next to me — this Pingone — cleared his throat and raised his hand.

'Yes?' asked the teacher.

Pingone, putting on a polite little voice, replied: 'Excuse me, Miss …'

And the teacher went: 'Yes?'

'Excuse me, Miss, may I ask you a question?'

'But of course.'

'So you think I'm a fucking nobody then, or what?'

She went all red and panicked: 'I — I — beg your pardon, sir …' (he'd started off so polite that she called him 'sir') 'I'm not sure I … why …'

'You're not sure my arse. You say we're all here,' continues Pingone. 'Well I'm here and you didn't even call my name. If I'm not here then I better go, right, Miss? My brother's waiting for me at the garage anyway, there's an engine needs fixing.'

Then he turned to face me: 'Am I right or am I right, you prick?'

I clearly wasn't in a position to disagree, on account of the beating I'd have got if I'd tried. And so it was that Pingone made such an impression on me on the first day of school that he became my best friend: teaching me how to do a wheelie and even giving me a few educational magazines exploring the mysteries of human reproduction.

Our friendship lasted two years, then he also started calling me a smart arse and I couldn't stand it. I mean, it's not like I wanted to put on airs, but I couldn't talk to him about the *poètes maudits* or how many grains of sand Catullus thought there were in the Libyan desert (answer: a fuck tonne). Right? So I stopped hanging out with him too, and then everyone really started to say I'd become unsufferable, and that I was going to a posh school because it was the only place I could get into a fight and come out in one piece. Or score three times in a row against the accountant's fat son, who only ever played in goal.

But let's be honest, it's not like things were great at the new school, either. My first Italian literature test was a disaster. My teacher, who was rumoured to be a Freemason, had a habit of calling us to his desk one by one in alphabetical order to return our essays, usually awash with blue and red pencil marks. When he got to me, he leafed through my test with a pensive look while I eagerly spied the seemingly immaculate pages. Eventually he folded the cover sheet with a swift movement and handed it to me. I had got an E. 'This is clearly not your work,' he said, in a perfectly neutral tone. 'What else can you expect from someone who lives by the railway tracks', he must have thought. I stood there like a lemon for a while, then went back to my desk. The following month he stood behind me, watching me like a hawk, for the entire duration of the test — maybe he expected me to have a stash of ready-made essays to copy, like some sort of word thief. That time he gave me an A- and offered me his wholehearted apologies.

He still kept marking my essays down though, because in his opinion I was 'a dangerous extremist'. One month my essays suggested I was a religious fanatic aggressively denouncing all transgressors, the next I'd turned into a staunch atheist who spoke in riddles — or rather, in obscure Nietzschean aphorisms. The truth is I was simply an impressionable teenager and a voracious reader: every book I read was a masterpiece to me, and like a magnet it shifted my entire ideological framework. Style-wise I was a chameleon too: I just imitated whichever author I'd read last. Sometimes I'd photocopy my essays and distribute them to my classmates, in the hope that my 'pamphlets' would stir up a student rebellion — like a homespun May '68. Needless to say, nothing ever came of it.

Luckily for him, my teacher only had to put up with my antics for one year, after which he was transferred to another school. I met him again several years down the line, when I'd already graduated from university. I was working a malodorous job as a stable boy at the racecourse in Follonica. He looked at my soiled, tattered blue overalls — hand-me-downs from my dad. In his eyes I saw commiseration — 'Poor boy, he could write but never really had a chance' — but also relief: 'He's better off where he belongs.'

Just like my reading and my writing, my body was also undergoing a turbulent fermentation process. It grew and transformed in a bizarre fashion: sturdy shoulders and footballer legs alongside thin, delicate hands — the hands of a pianist, or a writer — which would remain a constant source of grief as I got older. Later in life my body has periodically swelled and deflated, accumulating then losing fat, yet I have never been able to escape my blue-collar shoulders and white-collar hands. Not just my hands, but my wrists and my forearms are oddly slender and graceful and look out of place on my rough, ungainly frame — middle-class hands grafted onto a gargantuan working-class rootstalk. So much so that when I write, I feel my hands don't belong to me: they're somebody else's hands. They're strong hands though, and my fearsome 'donkey bite' was well known in the neighbourhood (a popular fighting technique throughout my childhood, which consisted of pinching and twisting a chunk of flesh on your enemy's leg, inflicting excruciating pain).

My shambling gait was known in my corner of Tuscany as *ciottolo* ('pebble' or 'stone') — leaden, lumbering steps that resonated heavily as I clomped around town. A rather rustic stride in short, exacerbated by my tendency to wear steel-capped safety boots that Renato was all too happy to hand down. By the time I got to the *liceo*, however, I had outgrown my original nickname of *ciottolo* and was universally known as 'egghead'. In the backwaters of Tuscany, anyone with academic ambitions was summarily ascribed the stereotypical features of the intellectual: a disproportionately large head and a Quasimodo-esque hunched back. The same fate had befallen the socialist anti-fascist Antonio Gramsci, so I didn't mind too much.

What I did mind, however, was being stuck in a slice of Tuscany hemmed in by two factories and the sea. Over the summer, my middle-class schoolmates would travel around Europe from Greece to the North Cape, coming back full of stories about London and Amsterdam and weed and aloof blond girls. My summer adventures, by contrast, were limited to the pub down the street from my house, which I'd visit with a metalhead friend of mine, the daughter of a train conductor. As for my English, it hadn't improved much since year 6. I'd never been further afield than the industrial estate in Livorno — except when, as a child, I'd accompany my father on his work trips to other such idyllic industrial estates and scenic chemical plants up and down the country.

And to think that, when I was twelve, my parents had inexplicably got me a subscription to the Italian Touring Club: I remember receiving a magazine with a photo of Lake Garda on the cover and a yellow card offering a discount for a local campsite. Discounts? Who needed discounts? The older guys I used to play football with could get into the posh campsites down in Punta Ala for free — they paid them to go, even. To trim lawns and empty bins, that is. Over the summer, hordes of tourists would descend on the Tuscan riviera expecting to be tended to, and fast, and ideally by people who didn't look *too* poor. Summers were a cacophony of 'There's no salt on my fried fish!' 'My pizza is cold!' 'How do I get to Cala Violina?' and 'Where's the club?'

It fell to my erstwhile friend Pingone — he of the bike wheelies — to answer the trickiest question of all. One day, as he walked out of the campsite gates to cut the grass along the fence, he was approached by a rather embarrassed motorist: 'Excuse me … do you happen to know where I might find some … er … I mean some … ladies of the night?' That's exactly what he said — 'ladies of the night'. My friend, astonished by such sophisticated terminology, gave him a puzzled look.

'Loose women, I mean,' clarified the man, opting for a lower register. Pingone removed his protective visor, leant against the car door, and looked him straight in the eye. When he spoke, he was so close that the guy's glasses fogged up: 'If loose is what you're after,' my friend said, proudly exhibiting his entire dentition, 'I've got a loose tooth right here at the back of my mouth, there may be something stuck in it as I just had a ham sandwich, but it's a good tooth. Will that do you, you think?' The poor guy released the clutch pedal and drove away as fast as he could.

My relationship with Renato, meanwhile, was becoming troubled. He didn't understand my lofty aspirations — didn't understand being a teenager for that matter, because that had been a luxury he couldn't afford: he'd been a child up until the age of thirteen, and then at fourteen he was already a grown man, bringing home the bacon. I, on the other hand, read books and fantasised about revolution while he worked like a dog in factories and building sites across the country. So I kept my distance — especially when, mooching about with my comrades, I'd spot him outside the sports bar nailing someone to the wall. 'Honestly, some people ...' I commented once to a fellow revolutionary (the accountant's son). 'They're just a bunch of old-school Stalinists,' he replied, 'better stay away from them.' So I steered clear of Renato and his sports-bar banter — steered clear of any banter to be honest. Engrossed in my books and ravaged by hormones, I rarely smiled and dark thoughts swirled around my head. My former friends, for their part, experienced no such existential dread: football, fights, women, and the steelworks were the four unshakeable cardinal points of their existence, paving the way to a glorious future which would see them married at twenty-two, with a mortgage and a baby on the way at twenty-four.

Renato grumbled. I'd stopped going to football matches with him — stopped playing altogether actually. He thought I'd gone soft. I wore my hair long and every now and again threw a tantrum, saying I hated maths and wanted to switch to classical literature instead. To someone like him, who worshipped at the altar of heavy industry and technology, the humanities were the preserve of pettifoggers, pundits, and priests. Of those, in short, who belonged to the 'wet' category — the way Renato described posh people who'd never done any manual work, and were therefore weak, spineless individuals you should be wary of. Francesca jumped to my defence: 'Don't say that, you'll hurt his feelings — he's so sensitive!' 'There's something wrong with the boy,' countered Renato. 'It's all those books he reads!'

The loudmouths down at the sports bar stoked my father's concerns. The friends Pa confided in were all in agreement: I was seriously ill. Some even alluded to signs of a latent homosexuality, which, according to them, was like one of those agricultural parasites: if you don't nip it in the bud, before you know it it's spread to the whole vineyard. The insinuating friends would inevitably end up pinned to the wall, but the seed was planted.

It came to a head one day when he spotted me outside

the church, just as I left the afterschool club. It may have been a working-class church, with a porch made from haematite extracted from the Island of Elba and forged in the ancient archduke's foundry; a church sitting between the Iron Museum and the library that used to be a blast furnace, with lumps of dross scattered around the courtyard; a church that was once run by rebel Jesuits and communist priests — but for all its proletarian credentials, it was a church nonetheless. That day, a beleaguered Renato and I squared off at the bottom of the corso, the main street that leads to the beachfront, like duelling gunslingers. He asked if I'd lost my mind for good. If by any chance I walked around with prayer beads in my pockets, too. I was tempted to mess with him and tell him I wanted to enter a seminary, but the thunderous look on his face suggested I should play it safe. In the end I replied — for the umpteenth time — that I went to the rebel Jesuits' afterschool club because of that girl he saw me with on the promenade.

He let it slide, but his friends kept teasing him: I used to be an excellent full-back, then stopper, then sweeper. I was set to go to the local vocational college. The glorious steelworks beckoned. Then one day, a strange wind blew me off course and I ended up in a *liceo*. The results were there for everyone to see: I'd stopped going to football practice, I didn't bully the younger kids, and now I'd even been spotted at the Jesuits' afterschool club. And in the library. Church and library: a terrible combination. 'It's all right for women and wimps with thick glasses — but Renato's boy? One hell of a full-back, he was. He could have gone places. He'd go in so strong he'd either

56

stop the ball or break your leg — shattered a few shins in his time, the kid. And now he's always in the library. Renato, have him seen by a doctor will you, your boy? There's something the matter with him.' Renato nodded. But in his heart of hearts he knew the truth: I was beyond help. I used metaphors.

In the end we made up, but still circled each other warily. He kept going on about football while I desperately attempted to emulate French existentialists. So thin that I appeared malnourished, with tufts of unruly hair sprouting from my head, I looked everywhere for unfiltered Gauloises, but had to make do with the much less glamorous Italian equivalent — unfiltered Nazionali — which gave me a nasty cough. I stopped leaving the house clutching *La Gazzetta dello Sport* and proudly exhibited the ultra-leftist daily *Il Manifesto* instead. On Sunday afternoons, just to wind me up, Renato would make me phone the local newspaper to check the amateur football league scores.

'Call the paper will you? Ask them how Ardenza did …'

'What? I'm not doing that! You can't just "call the paper" … they'll think I'm an idiot.' I read Camus and Sartre — I couldn't have journalists thinking I was an idiot!

'… Ah come off it, you big girl's blouse! What d'you think they'll do to you? Pick up the phone and ask them … Do it for your old man …'

Somehow he always pulled it off and I ended up calling the paper, mortified, picturing a busy news desk working on some Pulitzer-worthy investigative reportage. More often than not, however, the person on the other side of the phone was all too happy to oblige: 'Wanna know about those Ardenza pansies? Three-nil … and it was a home game! Cecina gave them a right old walloping. Sent them packing with their tails between their legs …' I would thank him and hang up, thinking I didn't belong there, that I was like Baudelaire's albatross, clumsy and awkward on a ship's deck. I had to start learning some languages and run away … learn them all, fast and badly — better to speak ten badly than a single one properly — and run away as far as I could. I dreamt of meeting new people, learning new things, and forgetting all about the Livorno & Grosseto amateur football league.

Despite all my struggles, I stuck it out and didn't lose my drive. It was no longer unheard of for working-class kids to study. And with a few sacrifices, every family could get a kid through uni, right? Be the first one to hang that much-yearned-for piece of paper on the wall. Who says you've got to toil and sweat like your forefathers? One step forward with every generation. Grandpa was a farm labourer and a bricklayer. Dad was an itinerant welder. And I was going to be an enlightened intellectual. With an actual degree, for fuck's sake! So I went off to study — and I didn't study like those who had to have concepts literally beaten into their heads to get a diploma in metalworking or what have you. I was motivated, hungry, and tough like a pack mule. I knuckled down to my schoolwork, forgetting all about football and fights. There was no more getting into trouble — I couldn't let my parents down now, could I? And after all, I thought (and Renato agreed) once I got that piece of paper I wouldn't need to fight anymore. I would put an end to the cultural hegemony of the ruling classes. And life would get easier.

Did it get easier? Did it fuck. Because even at school you got pigeonholed based on where you lived. There were the middle-class kids from San Luigi, the posh neighbourhood where the lawyers and doctors lived. There were those from the nearby villages or the inner-city old housing blocks, like me: the sons and daughters of factory workers and shopkeepers. Then there'd be the odd one or two from the countryside, repeating the year — they'd exile themselves to the bottom of the classroom and often disappear, having failed the year again.

As for the teachers, they came in all shapes and sizes too. My art teacher initiated us to the amazing work of Pasolini — but advised me to give up drawing because I was useless. My Italian literature teacher nurtured my voracious appetite for books — she was one of those educators who never need to maintain discipline because they love what they do so much that their enthusiasm is infectious. My maths teacher, on the other hand, enjoyed punishing us with homework — I was forever engaged in quixotic battles against logarithms and other such monstrosities. My English teacher lent me a Bob Dylan record once, but I preferred listening to the Sex Pistols.

Last but not least, one teacher introduced me to Ernesto Balducci, a communist priest from Mount Amiata. When Balducci delivered a lecture in the assembly hall I was blown away: he had a way of seeing things that was unlike any priest

I'd encountered, and he didn't speak like an intellectual. The son of a miner, his hands and ears were the size of dinner plates. After his lecture, Balducci stayed in town for dinner and the teacher invited me to join them. I accepted, but I was shy and awkward, unsure how to behave around someone who — I imagined — ate as little as an ascetic hermit. Instead, I watched dismayed as Balducci stuck his hands directly into the serving dish, hauled out a fistful of shellfish dripping with tomato sauce, stuffed it into his mouth and spat out the shells, making a mess of his frock. How could such a glutton call himself a communist priest? I wondered.

This episode (and Balducci himself) were quickly forgotten, until I was at university and heard he'd died in a car accident. Reading his biography, I learnt that as a child during the war, he'd eat only one meal a day. His mother would send him to the woods to steal chestnuts that she'd then boil and stuff in his pockets. Those boiled chestnuts were all he had to go on until the evening, when his father came home from the mine: in the darkness he'd spy the miners' acetylene lamps and warn his mother, who'd chuck the pasta in the broth for their dinner.

Suddenly it all made sense: that little boy grew up hungry — starving even. He wanted to live, read, study, and change the world. Table manners were for those who got three square meals a day, I thought. The son of a miner who'd survived his childhood living on chestnuts was exempt. And never mind manners actually — all that mattered was fighting injustice and oppression, whatever it took. That's why studying was important, studying with those principles in mind, studying like my pockets were stuffed with chestnuts too. Otherwise I'd only have been studying to get ahead, to compete, to beat the others to the punch — otherwise, I said to myself, you were only learning how to rip off thy neighbour. Studying with chestnuts in your pockets was different: it was for those who had centuries' worth of wrongs to right.

I graduated from school one bright July day, fully cooked. After that long summer, things somehow appeared bigger, more isolated, further away — 45 miles further away to be precise, seeing as I was now studying at Siena University. Everything was changing around me. Factory workers like my dad had lost their battle ten years before. Binmen were 'waste collection technicians'. Nurses were 'healthcare workers'. There were no bosses and masters anymore, only 'entrepreneurs'. Students were still protesting, flatly ignored by the wider public. The short-lived protest against the introduction of courses directly financed by private companies had fizzled out — university as an institution was changing, buckling under the pressure of the market: the ivory tower was crumbling. The professors who once studied working-class movements now taught the semiotics of luxury.

As for me, I couldn't even make sense of the students. In my new social life I discovered that wine had to be purchased in bottles — never bought in bulk cartons — and drunk in round, long-stemmed goblets — not tumblers. The goblet, moreover, had to be twisted this way and that, so you could fully appreciate the aromas, never mind drinking the actual wine. Next, you had to take a small sip and suck the liquid through your teeth making a strange hissing noise. Jesus Christ — can we drink it now? Nope. Spit it out. It's called 'wine tasting'. Guzzling down litres of red like my father and I used to do was, apparently, no longer in fashion. And then there were all the preliminary rituals ahead of the tasting itself, such as saying 'cheers' while looking each other in the eye. Every. Single. Time.

What the fuck was everyone always cheering about? I genuinely wondered, including that one time a guy from my linguistics course, the son of a famous barrister from Siena, invited me and an old friend of mine to a party at his house. We turned up to this ancestral mansion and I quickly realised we had only been invited so he could impress the girls: we were the oafs and he was the mild-mannered host. True to form, he immediately began fawning over the ladies while my friend and I gobbled up his wine in retaliation. He intercepted me as I was about to crack open a bottle of vintage Brunello di Montalcino: 'I'm sorry, this wine is meant for tasting.'

Oh god no, I thought, here we go again with the sniffing and the sucking and the spitting. 'Are you sure?' I asked him, 'because we're quite thirsty over here.'

'If you're thirsty you can drink water,' he replied. 'This is vintage wine, it requires … introspection. And you can't drink it straight away — you have to decant it and let it breathe overnight.'

Nice one, I thought, it's not like I'll still be around once it's done 'breathing'. So I smiled, locked my lips on the bottle, threw my head back and gulped down the vintage Brunello in one go. Deep, elegant and aromatic — seductively smooth. Then I wiped my mouth with the back of my hand, wiped my hand on my trousers, looked him straight in the eye and expressed my gratitude by way of a prolonged burp: floral, with strong spicy notes and a subtle mineral element — savoury, airy, and with a vaguely smoky aftertaste. At the climax of my performance — which was harmoniously drawn-out and ended in a powerful staccato — I bowed, waiting for my standing ovation. Needless to say, the host was beside himself and he kicked us out as my friend kept repeating, 'But have you tried the toilet paper in the loo? It's not like the one we've got at home ...'

And he was right — the toilet paper really was different. Everything was different. There was a whole world outside our neighbourhood, and we were the odd ones out: because that world was spellbinding, that world was trending, that world was winning. Gentrification — the latest myth peddled by the acolytes of progress — was the name of the game: out with the old! (and the poor). Entertainment, holidays, shopping. Wine tasting. Smooth legs, toned bodies, sleek interiors, fine dining. No more sacrifices, no more toiling, no longer shalt thou eat by the sweat of thy brow!

It was a bubble that would burst years later, leaving the country in tatters. As for me, I might as well have been living under a stone. I still watched football matches on muddy pitches. Other students talked about the Red Sea and the Swiss Alps, Ibiza and the Maldives — and I, as usual, answered with a burp (woody, with berry tones). Mostly, I just walked away. And if I absolutely had to say something, I told tales of my fearsome 'donkey bite'. Or of my strong toe-bounce. I told them I could keep my front wheel off the ground for ten seconds. I told them my pockets were full of chestnuts. They laughed, no doubt thinking I was an idiot.

To escape this hostile world of decanters and 3-ply toilet rolls, I took shelter in my books and fantasised about a solitary planet of my own, where a rose waited for me under a bell jar. Or perhaps not a solitary planet. Perhaps I fantasised about a horse-drawn cart with a Gatling machine gun, like in an old Peckinpah film.

I kept getting things wrong: politics, hobbies, even my degree. All my internal conflicts came to a head and I finally saw myself for what I was: a loser who knew nothing. I'd never experienced life beyond Livorno and Grosseto, except for a school trip to Rome and — most memorably — the infamous 'three-nighter', aka three days of assorted medical examinations and psychological tests you had to undergo in preparation for the National Service in Italy. To do it, I had been summoned to the barracks in Piazza Cestello in Florence. Afterwards, while the others headed to a brothel, I sneaked into a bookshop in town and stole a few books by my favourite Latin American authors.

At school I had fancied myself a budding intellectual — the champion of the working class, the scourge of the bourgeoisie: at university I felt like a fledgling who'd fallen out of his nest. I sat next to people who, aged five, had attended Foucault's linguistics lectures at the Collège de France in Paris. Others were practically hand-reared by Pier Paolo Pasolini himself. I was astonished. My credentials were limited to membership of every single socialist, workers', and football club in my little corner of Tuscany. *A voglia a be' ova, bimbo mio* — you've got to drink a few more dozen eggs, my son, Renato would have said. You've got a long way to go yet.

Disillusioned, I decided to move back home and commute to Siena when needed. I was ill at ease in this brave new world so full of opportunities — a flexible, fluid world that had replaced the world I knew. I didn't go to Ibiza or the Greek islands or to Val d'Isère. I wasn't what passed for witty in those days: I did not possess that sleek postmodern sense of humour — mellow, fruity, eminently palatable — even my irony was rustic and crude, it reeked of stables and cheap wine.

Once or twice a month I would go to Siena for the day to sit an exam or pick up a book from the library. In the end, I got my degree. On graduation day I was the only one who showed up alone, without any family or friends. The official photographer didn't even waste time on me: no flashes, no cheering as I shook hands with the Degree Committee.

I went back to my hometown with zero expectations. I started sending out CVs left, right, and centre, but the vacancies in my area (all fixed term, all requiring 3+ years' experience and paying next to nothing) were as follows:

> Unskilled cleaning staff
> Freight handlers
> Canteen staff
> Lorry drivers

> Salespeople
> Food preparation operatives
> Hairdressers
> Receptionists

All off the books, of course. Or hired as 'freelancers'.

I was advised not to mention that I had a degree on my CV. During the summer I worked in cafes, restaurants and beach clubs, but in winter there were no jobs to be found for love nor money. My awkward, delicate hands were put to use filling out endless application forms, once a week, at the job centre. I could see the *liceo* through the windows while I spoke to my employment adviser. I had once sat in those very rooms, my life a sequence of blank pages waiting to be filled with stories and dreams: I was a musketeer, half-Cyrano de Bergerac, half-Heathcliff. Now I spent my days filling out application forms for jobs that would probably never materialise, and when they did, it was almost worse. Cleaning up beaches every morning at six — first with a rake, then with an old spluttering machine. Opening the beach umbrellas and laying out the sun loungers. Making pizzas in a restaurant in the evening. Summer after summer, I watched the tourists have fun and relax while I worked like a dog: it seemed I was on the receiving end of life's own 'donkey bite'.

Pursuing my studies was out of the question — I was too tired to even read. I logged my hours in the notebook I once used for the bibliography of my dissertation. Plenty of hours of course, but poorly paid and off the books. You only 'got hired' if you had an accident at work. Never a day off. It was enough to drive you mad, or drive you away.

And away they all went, the bright minds of my generation, to Berlin, London, Barcelona, Paris. One day I bumped into an old friend outside the library: he was just back from Bristol. He said there were plenty of jobs over there — 'Shitty jobs like the ones we work here mind you, but better paid. And at least you'd be learning a new language.' And I'd get to see another slice of the world, one that wasn't bound by a rusty factory on the north side, and on the south side by the posh resorts of Punta Ala, where I used to mow lawns for a few pennies. Not anymore though, because some of my fellow lawn-mowers had become 'private contractors' (they too were 'entrepreneurs' now) — that is to say, not only did they pretend not to know me, but they'd actively call the police on me: in Italy, if they catch you with work tools and you're not a registered trader, they'll fine you on the spot. So much for The Rules.

So what the hell was I still doing there? I decided to try my luck in the UK. I bought a plane ticket, Renato and Francesca drove me to the airport.

'Let me carry your bag,' said Renato. 'It looks mighty heavy to me.'

Minimum wage, minimum life

England is a very good country when you are not poor.

George Orwell, *Down and Out in Paris and London*

Once upon a time, I was an off-the-books pizza chef in an Italian restaurant in Bristol. Flour. Heat. Back-breaking work. Not a single word of English learnt in the three months I spent locked up in the kitchen — unless you count the menu and Silver's Spanglish of course. A good chunk of my wages creamed off to pay for a bed in a lousy dorm. Working 24/7. Below minimum wage. No time off. No holiday pay. No sick pay. No National Insurance number. No overtime. Because we're all one big Italian family, right? Migrant graduates kneading dough like there's no tomorrow.

Go, they said. It's not like in the old days, they said. You are highly skilled 'expats', not desperate immigrants. Never mind those poor sods running away from poverty — you're 'looking for opportunities'. You'd be a fool to stay, they said. But come to think of it, had I actually left Italy? Because custom dictated that the rules of the motherland still applied in Italian restaurants the world over. Same boat, same standards. What employment contract? What minimum wage? You're expecting to be paid actual money, you ungrateful git? Some nerve you have! I gave you a roof over your head here in this foreign land! If you're not happy here's the door!

The door would have been nice actually — when we got a surprise restaurant inspection, the *padrone* pushed me straight out of the window. Done. He'd decided it was time for me to leave the Big Italian Family.

But there's a silver lining to every cloud and all that. Leaving that restaurant marked my actual arrival in the United Kingdom. After a few days I found myself at a bus stop in Bristol, ready for my first day of work as a bona fide Euro-immigrant: I had now formally joined the ranks of the glorious British proletariat. At 8.30 in the morning, a swarm of workers converged on the shopping centre: lanky, spotty teenage boys who'd left school at sixteen; or young sales assistants and fast-food servers in tightly pulled-back buns secured with hair claws, angrily flicking away their first cigarette of the day as they hurried through the revolving glass doors. I walked through a wide corridor flanked by dark, silent shops, then up the escalator. Empty tables everywhere. Behind the aluminium shutters that still encased the various fast-food counters, I could smell flavour enhancers and caged humans.

At the employment agency, I had been told to go to the food court and ask for the supervisor. And there she was — Annabelle. She scanned me from head to toe and smiled, then showed me where we Euro-temps — or 'agency people' as we were known — were supposed to get changed: a broom cupboard with piles of detergent cans everywhere. British employees had proper changing rooms with lockers, but we had to make do with this utility room that stank of cheap soap.

Annabelle handed me a raggedy, snot-yellow checked shirt and small black apron, a measly cloth and a spray cleaner: thus equipped, I would wipe tables. Also roaming the food court in search of tables to scrub were a Portuguese guy, three girls from Spain, and another guy from Greece: Erasmus students looking to earn a few extra pennies on weekends. Conversation among us was actively discouraged. We spent eight solid hours on our feet. 'Wiping tables' also included emptying the ashtrays in the smoking area, and emptying the food trays and stacking them on a trolley. I understood next to nothing and I couldn't speak to anyone — the Brits didn't even see us anyway. Fast food, self-service buffets. Everything stank of deep-fat fryers and synthetic flavours.

We weren't waiters, we were table-wipers: no talking, just walking — constant, relentless walking. No sitting down and above all NO TALKING — ever. The only approved terms were: ashtray, tray, bin, litter, table. That's all we needed. Verbs were the preserve of our supervisors, who used them to give us orders — as for us, we were only supposed to nod and get on with it. It was utterly dehumanising. I was on my feet, never stopping, never sitting down, never — ever — talking.

I looked at my watch — still two hours to go before the break. 120 minutes. 7,200 seconds of wiping grubby tables and emptying ashtrays. I made it to the break, exhausted — I reeked of cigarettes I hadn't smoked and my fingers were grimy with ketchup and mayo. I felt completely useless. Dejected. My legs ached. Somehow I held out until the end of the day. Beyond the glass walls the sun was setting, tinging everything around me with red. Little by little the food court emptied. Only a few tables were still occupied, peopled by specimens of British society who had been completely absent from my English textbooks, which were full of genteel old ladies and eccentric tweed-clad men: a sixteen-year-old girl was rocking her baby in a pram; a drunk guy had passed out on a table; a man in a suit looked at me with utter contempt.

The following day, Annabelle handed me a different shirt. It was dark blue, marking me out as a member of the cleaning staff: I'd been promoted to toilet maintenance duties. 'Staff shortage' was all the explanation I got. There was an abundance of table-wipers, but even the Erasmus students would draw the line at the badge of shame that was the blue shirt. My new colleagues, eager to see if I was tough enough to stay the course, made it clear to me from the start that we were the pariahs of the shopping centre, the untouchables, the Toilet Cleaners. 'You belong with us, I can tell,' a middle-aged woman told me. She had a wrinkly face crowned by a frazzled perm and stank of cigarettes. 'Wimps don't last long around here, you'll see.'

In hindsight, it was precisely in those loos — away from Annabelle's prying eyes — that I managed to learn some English. The smell wasn't great, but in there I found friends and mentors. And it's not like working at the mall's various burger joints was much better, anyway: watching English kids slave away at the counter was depressing. The stench of deep-fat fryers seeped into your pores, and no amount of showering could ever eliminate it. Punishing shifts. Standardised food — frozen, boxed, brick-shaped — served to rude customers after being defrosted, chopped, sliced, grilled, or fried by an assembly line of swearing serfs. Twenty-first-century culinary slavery. A cacophony of spluttering fryers, humming dishwashers, sizzling grills. And over that almighty racket, the implacable, unrelenting bell demanding ever faster food — a conditioned reflex that the miserable Pavlovian dogs behind the counter were powerless to resist. But there was always someone worse off, someone further down the ladder. And that someone further down the ladder was me.

It was Brian, my new colleague who couldn't pronounce his Rs, who explained to me how things worked. The lesson, needless to say, took place in the loos. Brian sat on a toilet — with his trousers on — while I listened, captivated, leaning against a sink. A very large man who weighed over 20 stone and looked a bit like an opera singer, Brian spilt over the toilet seat on all sides. It transpired he had already broken three such 'mediocre' toilet seats, i.e. the cheap plastic ones which, alas, had all but entirely replaced the 'far superior' ceramic and wooden seats.

They called him 'Pavawotti' because of his funny Rs — to be fair to him, they only happened when he got nervous or excited — and because of the way he looked. He sported a bizarre haircut — a centre parting with thick brown curls falling over his ears — and a goatee. His entire body jiggled and lolloped under the cleaners' dark blue shirt as he waddled around the shopping centre, his love handles wobbling in sync with his bouncing breasts and enormous buttocks. He'd often fashion a walking cane out of a broom wedged inside a dustpan, which — together with his funny Rs, his bow tie, and his braces — gave him an oddly aristocratic look, despite his decidedly common job (a cross between binman and plumber). And by his job, I also mean my job.

Brian, in short, was the most unappealing creature I had ever set eyes on. And the sweetest, most affable of men. This was his first lesson:

'My dear boy,' he spluttered, in an overly dramatic tone, 'what we do here is guawantee the perfect functioning of the dwaina … of the dwainage pi … pi … pipes.' (He stuttered a little, to boot.) He coughed, then carried on: 'Our supervisor will tell you we also have to patwol the shopping centre with our bwooms and dustpans and pick up chewing gum and food wappers. Fine. But that's not the point — those are definitely secondawy duties. We have a higher purpose, the smooth wunning of the entire building depends on us. Plumbing experts is what we are: we must avoid spillages at all costs!' I looked at him, confused — I didn't even have my pocket dictionary on me. Sensing my semantic predicament, Brian added: 'By "spillage" I mean the act of spilling.'

'I haven't a clue, Brian …' I replied, still puzzled.

'To spill …' he began as he rose, propping himself up on the broom and flicking away the giant bogey he had spent the past ten minutes locating in his beard, 'means to cause or allow something to fall, flow, or wun over the edge of a container, usually in an accidental manner,' he concluded, spluttering on 'accidental' and mimicking water flowing out of the toilet.

'Oh I get it — when the toilet is blocked and water comes out?' I said, proud as a teacher's pet.

'Exactly. Excellent. So — our customers are vewy nice people, well bwought up, and hence they like a clean, perfectly wiped postewior. I am quite knowledgeable on the matter. I know that you Italians, for instance, learnt to use the bidet fwom the Awabs. In some of our colonies, like India …'

'Ex-colonies, Brian,' I interrupted.

'Cowwect, ex-colonies … anyway, over there they use their left hand, which is twaditionally the impure hand, to wipe their buttocks — or sometimes a bucket, or a small shower — because toilet paper is vewy expensive. But here in the United Kingdom we make an excessive use of toilet paper, which is disastwous for the enviwonment. The enlightened few use a small towel soaked in water to clean their dewwière.'

Well, I never. Brian was the most learned person I'd come across in the UK. At least up until that point.

He was on fire. His lecture grew more riveting by the minute — the shopping centre toilets might as well have been the auditorium of a prestigious college.

'All this,' continued Brian, 'is to say that toilet paper often ends up clogging the toilet. Yet, compelled by biology, our clients must empty their bowels. At that point, because of their excellent upbwinging, they will pwomptly flush the clogged toilet and cweate a spillage.'

Brian kept rooting inside his nose as he spoke. He then wiped his moist forehead with the back of this hand and ran said hand through his hair. To me, Brian was like a maestro, albeit a somewhat revolting one, conducting his own personal bog symphony. While he lectured me on the sociology of human waste in the developed world, surrounded by a parade of shoes and male ankles peeking out from underneath the cubicle doors, customers walked in and out, accompanied by a soundtrack of flatulence and blasts of hot air from the hand-dryers. Doors swung open and closed. Flushed toilets emptied and their contents merrily gurgled all the way down to the septic tank. Unperturbed, he forged ahead with his discourse while I held my nose and expanded my English vocabulary to include a new faecal repertoire. Or should I say, 'wepertoire'.

Brian stopped to catch his breath, then resumed: 'When there's a spillage, no point mopping before you wemove the cause of the spillage. Come!' he said, leading me into a cubicle with a blocked toilet. 'Health and safety first: put out the yellow sign warning customers that the floor is slippewy. Now we surgically wemove the blockage. There are two options,' he continued, producing a filthy pipe. 'First you must lift the toilet seat so it doesn't get dirty. Then you punch thwough the blockage using this, making space for the water to flow.'

'And then the water pushes the toilet paper down.' I commented, thinking back to Renato's hydraulics lessons.

'Exactly, young man! Exactly! Bwilliant explanation.'

Brian had found an acolyte.

'Would you like to do the honours?' he asked, handing me the filthy pipe.

'If I must …'

'Well I'd pwefer to do it myself actually. Vewy kind of you to give me the opportunity …' He paused and looked at me, then carried on in a conspiratorial tone: 'I actually have my own personal method — much maligned, alas, by other members of our club.'

'Our club?'

'Other toilet cleaners!'

'Oh, okay.'

He winked and his mouth broadened into a big grin: 'Twicks of the twade — Bwian's magic touch! But I'll let you in on my little secwet …'

I couldn't wait to find out what the secwet was.

'You see, to get the water flowing, all you have to do is lift the clump of toilet paper.'

Then he plunged his arm elbow-deep into the clogged toilet with a rotating movement, and re-emerged clutching a blob of sodden toilet paper that melted in his hand.

'Listen!' he ordered authoritatively, pointing to the toilet bowl. Kneeling on the floor, he propped up the mop against the cubicle wall and cupped his hand behind his ear, like a footballer basking in the glory of a roaring stadium. As we waited, he started fingering a dirty thread from the mop, serene and blissful as a little cherub — until a gurgling, sucking draining noise sealed his triumph. Wielding a toilet brush, Brian stood up and began singing an aria from Puccini's

Turandot: '*Dilegua, o notte! / Tramontate, stelle! / Tramontate, stelle! / All'alba vincerò / Vincerò / VINCERRRRRRRÒ!*' I watched, powerless, as specks of murky water from the toilet brush lashed the mirrors I had only just wiped.

'Bravo, maestro!' I said to him. Grinning at his imaginary audience, he bowed his head, then tossed the filthy blob of loo roll back into the now perfectly functioning toilet. A strip of wet paper was still clinging to his forearm. He flushed the toilet again, stroked his satyr-like goatee and straightened his bow tie:

'Nicely done, hey?'

I didn't know whether to laugh or vomit.

Brian removed the yellow 'slippery floor' hazard sign and picked up his broom: 'Lovely job, if I say so myself. Now I'm off to Marks & Spencer's.' He was so proud of his success, positively beaming with joy. 'But don't imagine you'll be able to do that stwaight away, young man. It takes years of pwactice. Ancient Bwistolian cwaftsmanship!'

I looked in the mirror. Vomit was definitely gaining the upper hand over laughter. The fetid vapours emanating from the cubicles combined with the synthetic fragrance spritzed from the ceiling to create a sugary, nauseating scent that made the air unbreathable. To Brian, it probably smelt like roses. To me it smelt like death and cheap cologne. I had to get out, fast.

I opened the door and breathed in clean air. Relief. Short-lived relief, however, because Annabelle was waiting for me outside the toilets.

'Your English is improving,' she said, smiling.

'Thank you, Annabelle. Yes, it's getting better. I practise a lot ...' I replied, thinking it was a genuine compliment. I soon realised it was a trap. Poisonous, vicious sarcasm.

'But you see, this isn't a school. You're not here to learn a new language. You're paid to wipe and sweep.'

Annabelle couldn't go into the gents' and she knew the male cleaners congregated there to talk about sports or personal matters, away from CCTV cameras and supervisors.

'You should only be in the toilets for the time it takes you to check there are enough paper towels and wipe the mirrors ...'

'I'm sorry, there was a ... spillage!' I said, proudly exhibiting my newly acquired vocabulary.

'I wasn't finished. I know there's a spillage — I can see water coming out from under the door! So mop it all up straight away! And from now on I want to see you sweeping and picking up litter non-stop from Gap to Marks & Spencer's. Now go. Chop-chop!'

For the shopping centre workers, Gap and M&S represented the North and South pole. In the middle was the food court, where young Brits or Erasmus students slaved away for the minimum wage. We were the true pariahs: working-class Brits with various troubles or Euro-losers like myself. Constantly monitored by Annabelle on the CCTV cameras, we were doomed to roam the corridors all day at a steady pace.

According to the views circulating on the secret bog grapevine, Annabelle was universally considered a bitch.

She knew that of course, and in response she was constantly breathing down our necks. The rumours had started after Kate was fired following a period of intense bullying by Annabelle. It took me a while to figure out who Kate was. One day, I spotted an elderly woman who looked like the stereotype of the English old lady to me — she wore thick glasses, a bit of rouge on her pale cheeks, and had tight, dark-grey curls. I imagined her sipping tea from a dainty little cup in a plush sitting room with floral wallpaper.

Instead, she made a beeline for the staff room and walked in, closing the door behind her. I ran after her to explain that the ladies' toilets were on the other side of the food court, but when I opened the door I was amazed to see all my colleagues gathered around her. Everyone was hugging and cheering her. I was introduced as 'the one who replaced you', which felt rather awkward. I paused, unsure what to say, but she hugged me too and warned me I had better do a good job cleaning those toilets.

Kate, it turned out, used to be the oldest employee at the shopping centre. She could have retired but chose to keep working — her family lived far away and she got bored at home by herself, so she didn't at all mind wiping mirrors and mopping floors to keep in shape. Because she was so old, however, she was often off sick — so Annabelle received orders from the Powers That Be to make her life hell, and in the end Kate caved in and resigned. And who did they hire in her place? A young temp worker with no rights. One who can't claim sick pay if he catches the flu. Your humble narrator, in short.

And so there we were, looking at each other: the old English lady with a proper employment contract and the young Euro-immigrant, the temp with a rubbish agency contract. And what do you think she went and did next? She said goodbye to everyone, hooked her arm around mine, and took me for a walk around the shopping centre. I could feel her frail bones rubbing against my T-shirt. Her voice was sweet but steady, her English clear and easy to understand. I told her that.

'But of course, darling. I had to learn it too, you know?'

'Wait, you're not English?'

'English? Never! I'm Irish, darling — but don't tell anyone, only our cleaner friends know, and they keep their mouths shut. That's why my English is so good — I used to have an Irish accent, which wasn't very well received around here in the seventies, let me tell you. So I learnt the Queen's English from a TV show called *Upstairs, Downstairs*, and now no one can tell where I'm from! I sound just like one of those posh ladies, don't I? I'm off to Alicante soon — shall I bring you with me?' she winked. 'Ah well, we'll have to make do with getting on Annabelle's nerves ... by the way, how is that witch treating you?'

Kate asked me how I got by as an immigrant in the UK. And she began telling me her own stories, one by one. How she'd travelled from Northern Ireland to London in the sixties. Her Irish accent. Her violent husband. Pints of stout, black eyes, a daughter she raised by herself. Coming home to piles of dirty clothes and dirty nappies and a crying, colicky baby and more beatings. Finally, a divorce — and many other such terrible things. My own misadventures paled in comparison. Even Annabelle's eyes slowly burning a hole in my back seemed a mere trifle, a fly I could just swat away with my hand. Suddenly my head was spinning, and the tables and the garish fast-food signs were spinning too, and the food court disappeared, and in its place was a dusty square in a town in the Wild West — there, in the glaring light of high noon, I saw Annabelle in the middle of the square, ready for our duel. I could feel Kate's warm, frail body next to me — rough and solid like old bark, with a vague scent of tea.

Then Kate and I danced across the shopping centre with our brooms like Fred Astaire and Ginger Rogers, our shiny black shoes gliding effortlessly on the smooth tiles, magically sweeping away greasy food wrappers discarded by rude customers. And then Kate's broom was an umbrella, and like Mary Poppins she flew us up, up above the shopping centre roof, and from a wonderful rooftop terrace we saw green hills emerging from the mists over Bristol. Then out of her bag materialised cigarettes and cans of beer, which we sipped with our cracked lips. And then, and then, we rested our tired, underpaid-workers' feet on that shopping centre that devoured our time, that sleeping dragon of plastic and plaster. Oh Kate, how I wish we could have worked together — what a team we would have made!

The dream lasted a split second. But when I landed back in the food court I returned Annabelle's gaze with the steely determination of a wandering gunslinger. I wasn't afraid of her anymore. It must have rattled her because as of that day she

got off my case — or at any rate, things got easier for me.
Annabelle gave me a new task and started acting all genial
and gracious with me, which I couldn't stand: every time she
intercepted me on one of my endless patrols up and down the
corridors, she'd smile and say 'see you later, alligator', honestly
expecting me to reply 'in a while, crocodile'. Revolting. I always
refused to play along, which is why — among other reasons
— she never liked me. I mean, can you imagine what my dad
would have said if he saw me play alligator and crocodile with
the boss? I still had some dignity left, and I couldn't betray The
Rules.

At any rate, despite ignoring Annabelle's fake smiles and
idiotic rhymes, I was promoted to a new role: twice a week
I was to don a red sweater, gather the bins in the basement
and help hook them to the bin lorry. Meanwhile, I'd met two
Spanish girls — Pilar and Rocio — at an evening English
course. Their house parties were full of Spanish guests, mostly
Erasmus students. There were care packages from home full
of delicacies: Serrano ham, Manchego cheese, olives. We'd
buy bottles of terrible red wine and mix it with Coke to make
calimocho: a sugary concoction that masked the acidic taste of
sulphites and got you unexpectedly drunk. Pilar and the girls
could only cook one thing, but they had it down to perfection:
huge onion and potato tortillas. I'd only go to their parties on
Saturdays, as afterwards I couldn't get up in the morning.

I remember meeting a blond Spanish girl I really fancied
there. We didn't have much in common: she was a middle-
class Erasmus student destined for a brilliant career; I was an

Untouchable. We spoke a little, but conversation only drove us further apart. She had emerald green eyes the colour of waves breaking against white cliffs. I could have drowned in those eyes. When I told her I cleaned bogs for a living, however, she stopped smiling. Might as well get back to work.

Aside from issuing orders, the only sanctioned form of interaction between management and staff was the Staff Meeting. We'd all stand in a big circle, each team recognisable by its colours: yellow checked shirts for the food court workers; dark-blue shirts for the toilet cleaners; green polo shirts for the maintenance team; red sweaters and dirty high-vis jackets for the basement workers. Only team supervisors were allowed to speak, mostly to say everything was running smoothly, and at any rate only after the manager or the deputy manager were done with their little speech.

Charlene, the deputy manager, came across as easy-going and casual even by Italian standards, while the manager, Clive, was in his mid-forties, slim and elegantly dressed, with a floppy fringe. Renato would have instantly dismissed both as 'wet'. 'Bunch of drips, the lot of them,' he used to say: liquid people. People you couldn't trust. And Clive and Charlene were indeed wet through and through. Moist. Positively diluted.

For all their affable manner and informal style, they always spoke first and no one ever dared contradict them. The staff, of course, had no say in anything — let alone 'agency people' like myself. If you complained — the cheek! — you'd get fired on the spot: 'It appears the gentleman here needs some time off.' And as the Rule goes, if they call you sir, stick your arse to the wall and watch out: there'll be a letter in the post soon telling you not to even bother picking up your things, as the uniforms are the property of the shopping centre anyway. I'd seen it happen many times. Workplace bullying was really bad there — all it took was for Annabelle to drop a hint that someone was about to get the sack, maybe because they took too many breaks, or they were caught skiving. Everyone would immediately start bad-mouthing the person in question — suddenly they weren't a 'team player', they were selfish, they didn't take pride in wiping tables or ensuring the smooth running of drainage pipes. They didn't care about Our Brand. After a while, the beleaguered worker would get a one-way ticket for the magical world of unemployment, without so much as a peep from their former colleagues.

The bog grapevine was where you'd usually hear if someone was headed for the chop. All manner of stories — real, fake, unverifiable — would originate in the cleaning-staff storage room, circulate through the extractor fans or the plumbing system, or perhaps the sewage pipes themselves, and slowly spread across the shopping centre. The most alarming news doing the rounds lately concerned Brian: according to our colleagues he was utterly miserable. He still smiled and said 'enjoy!' — especially when he plunged the fetid rubber pipe or his own arm into a clogged toilet — but his eyes had lost that sparkle, and you could tell he wasn't actually enjoying himself. I heard that he was lonely and had heart problems, that he subsisted on fish and chips and watched unfunny 1950s comedies every night. Even his bow tie was looking wonkier by the day, and his worn-out braces struggled to hold up his enormous trousers.

Only a magazine I'd salvaged from a bin one day managed to put a smile on his face: it featured an illustrated article entitled 'The Upside-down World'. The illustrations reproduced what looked like ancient lithographs with archaic-sounding captions, which I deciphered with the help of the images themselves. First vignette: a little girl breastfeeds her mother and a little boy educates his father. Second vignette: the lady of the house serves dinner while the footman eats at the table. A chained man barks at his dog. A dog goes hunting and his man brings back a quail. Hens fight over a cockerel, and the cockerel lays eggs. The king is on foot and his squire on a horse. A nobleman begs and a beggar gives him a shilling. A farmer shears a pig and a cart pulls its oxen. Rivers flow up the mountains. A snail outruns a horse. Some hens hang a fox. The dumb speak. The lame run.

That article made a strong impression on me. I spent hours daydreaming about the upside-down world, whilst not picking up any litter at all. The litter-picker saunters around the shopping centre while customers pick up discarded burger boxes. The pizza chef sits down to dinner and the restaurant owner makes pizzas. Factory workers like my dad have a spa day and the bosses toil and sweat by the blast furnace. Tourists harvest olives in the fields of Tuscany while I go skiing in the Swiss Alps.

Except I can't ski, so I end up trashing the whole fucking resort in frustration. London Bridge is falling down, bitches.

Iron and steel will bend and bow,

Bend and bow, bend and bow,

Iron and steel will bend and bow,

My fair lady.

But alas, that distorted nursery rhyme didn't accomplish much by way of power redistribution. That particular brand of white magic required a secret ingredient — collective action — and my enemy was too mighty an opponent, its evil powers too great.

I realised this one day, and my mood suddenly darkened. I was on my way to the basement, carrying bins filled to the brim with dirty nappies from the baby changing room. Annabelle glared at me — she was in a foul mood that day and couldn't bear to be around any of the staff. On my usual route through the basement, I caught a whiff of rotten fish and putrid seaweed. Intrigued, I decided to follow the unlikely scent trail. I walked a fair while, covering my nose with a hankie when the stink became unbearable. I could hear people chanting strange words — a chorus of sorts, a sinister summoning: 'Give us a sign, oh Lord! A sign from your Dark Cave! Cthulhu! Your wish is our command!'

I had no idea what was going on, but the voices grew louder and louder as I crept along the wall, trying to make as little noise as possible. Then I turned a corner and what I saw froze the blood in my veins. Shaking, I jumped back and hid behind a pillar, but the chanting continued a few steps away from my temporary shelter. I risked a glance and saw Annabelle, Clive and Charlene kneeling before a nook where a figurine stood. It was the same abominable squid-like idol I'd seen in the pizzeria in Bristol, albeit far larger in size. A few credit cards and a photograph of a woman were arranged around it like votive offerings. The woman looked strangely familiar, like a childhood memory buried deep in the recesses of my mind. Tall, gaunt and severe, she sported a strawberry-blonde puffy hairdo and a sober suit, and a belt made of skulls shone around her waist. Her mouth was wide open and her tongue stuck out in a ghastly grimace. Glorious and terrifying, feared and venerated, she had multiple arms and each of her hands was lifted in a different ritual gesture. Her disciples' mantra was at once a symbol of power and punishment, discipline and prosperity, carrot and stick. And then I knew who she was. Maggie the Destroyer. The Wicked Witch of the West.

It all felt a bit ridiculous and I suppressed a hysterical laugh, but it bounced back from my stomach leaving an acrid taste in my mouth. I gagged. The noxious fumes emanating from the slimy walls of the basement infiltrated my lungs, fear gripped my chest and ran through my veins. My knees buckled. Huddled on the floor behind the pillar like a terrified child, I wiped my mouth with the back of my hand — a thick slimy substance oozed from my nose.

Annabelle, meanwhile, continued her incantation: 'There is no such thing as society. There are only individuals,' while the other two repeated: 'Your wish is our command!' Then, suddenly, silence. I don't know how long it took me to pluck up the courage to stick my head out from behind the pillar. When I did, the place was empty. No Annabelle, no Clive or Charlene, no Maggie the Destroyer.

Traumatised, I got up and ran. Who would believe me if I told them what I saw? I wasn't even sure *I* believed what I saw — my brain felt like a blown engine, pistons madly firing. Snippets of memories came back to me. Wasn't that the same rotten fish smell that haunted me in the pizzeria? And hadn't I begged the very ghost of Margaret Thatcher to help me find a job in the UK? Mocked that ghost even, with my stupid pizza Margherita mantra? I knew I wasn't supposed to believe in ghosts, but it's hard to remain sceptical in a place like Britain, which is positively infested with them. And hadn't I been warned, come to think of it — all those stories I'd heard on the bog grapevine and dismissed as urban legends, gallows humour, baseless superstition — dark tales of obscene rituals, human sacrifices of unsuspecting employees, secret ceremonies in containers shipped from China … I never believed any of that stuff, obviously.

But now I wasn't so sure. Clive and Charlene and their cheerful 'Good morning, team!' at the daily staff meeting — what were they hiding? Why did we have such a high turnover? Why did so many people seem to just vanish? Where did they end up? Suddenly I couldn't stand Annabelle looking at me: I felt her eyes digging into my skull as though she were reading my mind.

Things took a turn for the worse a few days later, when Brian got the sack. When I walked into our 'changing room' everyone was looking rather forlorn. 'Bad news,' they announced. 'What bad news?' I replied, a friendly smile dying on my lips.

'It's Brian ...'

'Did something happen to him?'

'Yeah ...'

'Is it his heart?'

'His heart? No, he got fired!'

'Fired?!' I couldn't believe it. 'Did they fire him?' I asked again.

'Yes ... Ridiculous!'

'Where is he now?'

They'd seen him burst into the gents' in tears. Inside I found a row of puzzled faces staring at one of the cubicles. The door was open. Brian was sat on the toilet with his pants and boxer shorts pulled down to his ankles, talking to himself and whistling random tunes. Every now and again he'd throw in a few opera arias for good measure. He'd taken off the dark-blue T-shirt and his vest was bunched up to expose his almost hairless belly. He saw me and waved. He kept talking — to me, perhaps, or to no one in particular — his eyes were completely vacant.

It was Brian's last day at work. His positive attitude was like an amulet warding off the dark forces emanating from the sinister idol, which seemed to feed off our very own flesh and blood. In my increasingly turbulent and apocalyptic dreams, a gigantic naked demon sat on the shopping centre as on his throne, crushing a pile of customers that were still clutching their shopping bags. The bodies were then crammed into the escalator as though onto a conveyor belt. Steel claws rammed them into the food court where the devil belched out fire and brimstone onto them. Meanwhile, drunk on proletarian blood, faithful servants bearing the mark of the Beast flung the screaming shopping centre workers off the food court balcony and straight into the mouth of the devil. Once the Beast was sated, the remaining bodies were torn to pieces and the human limbs bunched up with barbed wire: thousands of arms and legs that clogged the shopping centre toilets until blood spilt out of every hole. Then I would wake up to Annabelle's voice calling me back to reality: 'Grab your mop and clean up that mess!' Compliant, I went to the toilets to fill up my bucket, but blood gushed out of the taps too.

Screaming, I woke up — this time for real. My sheets were drenched. It was still dark and I was safe in my bed; it was just a nightmare. But I couldn't go on like that: I was going mad, there was no way around it. I had to leave before it was too late, before Annabelle turned on me.

Before I lost my mind for good.

Know your place

We perceived that we were not splendid inhabitants of a splendid world, but a crew of underpaid workmen grown squalidly and dismally drunk.

George Orwell, *Down and Out in Paris and London*

Stonebridge in Dorset wasn't that bad actually — limestone walls and white cliffs. I liked the stone cottages and the pier at the bottom of the bay, the cornflower-blue shutters and the large sash windows designed to capture the cold light of the Channel and funnel it into the houses. I walked along the beach, determined to put my demons behind me. The sea spray slapping me on the face reminded me of home, except for the temperature, which was still low in late spring.

Putting one foot in front of the other, I pressed on along the coast and past a rocky cove framed by a grey strip of sand. Here and there, a few seaweed-covered stones marked the tidal range. I stopped to catch my breath. This is the place, I thought: beyond a park and a hedge I could see a nice, friendly-looking red brick building. Behind it sat another building which I later learnt housed the sports centre, the large canteen, and the laundry. And then there was a tennis court, a football pitch, a trampoline, a shed where all the sports equipment was kept, and further back still, classrooms and offices and rows of twee wooden bungalows where the teachers slept, and the director's house, Cthul Manor, a Victorian mansion perched on top of a stern hill. Finally, hidden from view and a fair distance from everything else — exiled, quarantined — were the shabby kitchen staff dorms where, according to the instructions I was given over the phone, I had to report for duty.

My supervisor was already waiting for me. He seemed like a reasonable, low-key type, a bit stressed maybe. At any rate, my new life as a kitchen skivvy wouldn't officially start until the Monday, so I had the rest of the day to myself. I slept a bit, and that evening I met one of the teachers — a genuinely lovely girl who invited me round for dinner with her colleagues. She introduced me to her friends, who were somewhat less enthusiastic to meet me once they figured out I worked in the canteen: there was the blond hippie intellectual who only talked about travelling, and the sporty curly-haired economics graduate who planned to join the Clipper Round The World Race before coming back to find a job in the City and repay his student loan. A girl wanted to be an architect in Cape Town, another two stocky yet sporty types played hockey — which in the UK is played on grass, I learnt. Then there was the curvy, glamorous blonde whose boyfriend was a professional climber and yet another blonde, from Sussex, with a very posh accent.

We talked about this and that, and I listened to their stories of gap yahs and bargain flights and the amazing fish curry they had in Goa, and ten pound notes slipped into passports to bribe the customs officers in those corrupt countries that, you know, it's great they're independent now, but they're so dysfunctional …

The following morning I woke up at seven and as indicated in my contract I headed to the canteen, where I found a bunch of nutters hoovering up Rice Krispies and milk. One by one, their sleepy faces drew nearer and introduced themselves: Ian, Tim, Ross the supervisor, and Fatty Boy. My new colleagues. They weren't much to look at, but it's not like I had to sleep with them. One of them was preparing the breakfast special: an enormous spliff, so long it seemed to defy gravity. 'This is for our break,' he said, winking at me. 'White Widow from the Netherlands — indoor production. Mental stuff.' Well fuck me sideways, now we're talking. What was I thinking, slaving away in Bristol? I should have come straight here.

After a while the kids began pouring into the canteen like zombies, so we hid the spliff and put on our best Employee-Of-The-Year smiling faces to greet them, including Tim (muscly, shaved head) and the lanky one they called Fatty Boy, who looked like he was fresh out of rehab. We donned the black aprons and white paper hats that identified us as kitchen staff — kitchen assistants, to be precise — and began setting the tables. The guys explained that each table had to have its butter and jam and marmalade and water and milk. Then we had to get behind the counter and fetch the vats of glutinous baked beans, and toast the sliced bread, and fry the sausages — both the pork and the soy kind — and of course the bacon, dripping in fat then rapidly congealing on the plates.

Meanwhile, hordes of screaming children kept pouring into the canteen one class after the other, and the teachers screamed too. All the kids had to say Thank You, and to each kid you had to reply Cheers or You're Welcome — thousands and thousands of soul-destroying thankyous and cheeeeers, but refusing got you fired if you were a grown-up and sent home if you were a kid. Then the manager came in to tell off Ian (the chubby, lairy one) for being late again — 'Listen, you've got to be on time, okay?' 'Sorry.' 'And take off that bloody eyebrow piercing while you're at it, will you.' I sensed Ian was about to reply that his eyebrows were none of the manager's fucking business, but he didn't. Meanwhile another batch of kids had replaced the first one: these were even louder and rowdier, and the teachers barked like drill sergeants. Finally, a group of five older teenagers looking distinctly like young offenders walked in, accompanied by just as many teachers (or guards) with a retired-boxer look about them.

It was with this last group that we played football after breakfast — they were great fun. None of us were any good to be honest, least of all your humble narrator: I was older than the rest and didn't have the stamina anymore. But I was happy: I'd finally reconciled with football. Because once upon a time, when I was a scrawny little kid, football wasn't a sport to me, it wasn't something I did for fun: it was basic survival, a way to keep my head above water. On the streets where I grew up, you were either good at kicking heads or good at kicking the ball. Middle-class kids don't *need* football — they can watch it on

TV if they want to, or maybe they prefer tennis or fencing or what have you. Either way, it's just for fun. It's a 'leisure activity'. But if you're always out playing because your parents are at work and you hang out with packs of feral kids, frustrated by life and walloped at home, trust me —- decent dribbling skills will stand you in good stead. They'll keep you out of scuffles and earn you the respect of your friendly neighbourhood thugs. Even off my game as I was, a couple of well-timed feints and a top corner goal earned me instant stardom in that kingdom of pots and pans. It was not with my degree that I impressed my fellow master chefs — the kitchen staff syndicate, the Stonebridge Kitchen Assistant Nasty Kommittee or SKANK, as they called themselves, like a bunch of would-be gangsta rappers with rapidly expanding beer bellies under their blue uniforms and football shirts — but with my feet.

I hadn't kicked a ball in eons. My football studs used to be my most prized possession: I'd spend hours greasing the leather with warm suet and replacing the studs with a spanner — the metal ones gave you better grip on mud in winter, and the rubber ones were for spring, when the mud turned to dust. Then the Heysel Stadium disaster changed everything — I was only a child, but I'll never forget that evening: the terrifying images of supporters being crushed to death in a human stampede.

After that, I kept playing in the local junior leagues for a couple more years, but the magic was gone: disappointed by neighbourhood strikers and *Serie A* champions alike, I quit playing for good. I still remember the morning after the disaster

— I bought my usual *La Gazzetta dello Sport*, and my Italian teacher asked me to explain to the class what the papers said. The papers said Liverpool's hooligans were to blame. Later we learnt that the stadium was falling to pieces, but anyway, the general consensus was that English hooligans were animals.

In Italy, the Iron Lady was widely credited with putting an end to 'the English Disease' of hooliganism: undercover cops, named seats instead of generic spots on the terraces, CCTV cameras, etc. Talking to my new associates during our break, however, I learnt that English football fans had a different perspective on the matter. As far as they were concerned, they were pushed out not by police truncheons but by the price of season tickets, which skyrocketed after the big clubs started building new stadiums. Belligerent, rowdy, angry blue-collar fans had been priced out of football matches and replaced with more mild-mannered (and deep-pocketed) supporters. Then private media groups scooped up the broadcasting rights and the poor sods had to fork out a fortune to even watch the matches on TV.

Violence in stadiums had reduced, fair enough, but there was a lot less genuine passion as well — maybe some aspects of old-school football fandom didn't deserve to be obliterated by the advent of pay-per-view TV and betting shops and bloody VIP boxes. Either way, I wondered, where did all the hooligans go, since they weren't allowed into stadiums anymore? Luckily for them, the UK's booming rave scene welcomed them with open arms. That must have been a sight to see: waifish Cambridge students hugging pot-bellied forty-something plumbers with brawny arms covered in scars and West Ham tattoos, all merrily popping amphetamines in a field like there was no tomorrow.

As I visualised this scene, Ross — that rare thing, a working-class supervisor — snapped me out of my football-induced reverie: time to go, the manager's on our case. Before we went back in, however, he showed me *The Sun*'s page 3, featuring Emily from Bournemouth: 'Look at those jugs!' Ross was a very outgoing type, and he talked exclusively about sex or other bodily functions. His bugbear was not being able to find condoms in his size: the matter was so serious he had resolved to make a formal complaint. Making a complaint, I was beginning to understand, was a time-honoured British pastime: I'd seen it at the shopping centre where I used to work too, where asking to 'speak to the manager' was the perfect ending to a day of frenzied shopping.

Ross wanted to complain to Durex on account of their condoms being too small, 'and one even broke for fuck's sake … so like, if I end up with a sprog then what? Durex help pay for nappies, do they? I'm serious mate, they've got to get their act together.' Ross asked for my help to write the complaint because — he maintained — my spelling was surely better than his, seeing as at school he'd mostly learnt to smash heads. I agreed, and he began dictating his long list of grievances.

It had been a while since I'd taken dictation. At school, dictation exercises were largely used as punitive measures, and I hated them. I remember one PE teacher in particular — a bit of an oddball — who'd usually brush off our impertinence with a few inappropriate jokes, but when he was in a foul mood, instead of sending us out to play football he'd subject us to cruel dictation exercises. Out of his cursed locker he'd extract an enormous anatomy tome with crinkled yellow pages and begin reading a random passage on the human skeleton out loud, barking like a gun dog on a hunt. His reading was often interspersed with the most atrocious profanities, dutifully transcribed by us pupils. Meanwhile, next door an appalled nun tried in vain to persuade the hardened souls of the local working-class kids to embrace Our Lord Jesus Christ. I'm pretty sure that had a nun been at hand while Ross dictated his complaint, she would have been just as appalled.

When we finished I was surprised to see it was still light outside even though it was approaching 10 pm. We played football again, chucked some leftover bread at Dorset's enormous crows, then went back in and did the dishes — and to my astonishment, we just left them to dry, unrinsed. Five hours to log on my timesheet. Knackered, I gulped down a few lagers and went to bed, where I lay awake imagining the suds dripping off the pots in the canteen, slowly, in the dark.

The following day our work routine was exactly the same, except for the manager popping in to tell us *all* off: apparently, someone had been watching porn in the staff room next to his office earlier that morning, around the time the teachers usually came in. We were also reminded that illegal substances were absolutely not permitted on the premises. We pretended not to understand and walked away shaking our heads. 'Any more of that and I'll report you to the big boss!' he concluded.

The 'big boss' was the director who lived in the big Victorian mansion on top of the hill, Cthul Manor. No one knew who he was: he was a recluse and never mixed with us mere mortals. There were all sorts of rumours circulating about him — that he had a serious degenerative disease, that he was crippled and disfigured, that he couldn't stand the daylight. I ventured up the hill once, but as soon as I approached that sombre building a cold, hostile wind arose, seemingly out of nowhere. Sensing imminent danger, I felt shaky and my eyes filled with tears, while sweat dripped from my forehead and mucus oozed out of my nostrils. All my various saline secretions met and coalesced in my mouth. I could feel fear crystallising on my skin. Then, as suddenly as it had appeared, the blast of cold air vanished, replaced by an eerie silence — it was over. Somehow, I was now only a few metres from the kitchen staff dorms. I had no idea how I'd managed to get back down the hill, but I was sure as hell never going to wander anywhere near Cthul Manor again.

Determined to banish that bitter taste from the back of my mouth, I rushed into a pub. There I met Tim, one of my fellow kitchen assistants, and we started buying rounds. Pint by pint, my troubles seemed to fade away: I followed my esteemed colleagues' lead and squandered my meagre earnings on beer and slot machines.

Membership of the SKANK gang was in fact contingent on strict adherence to a specific set of social norms, which included consuming gallons of lager and prowling the clubs in search of willing girls. Girls in fancy dress, orange girls,

girls squeezed into microscopic tops, fearless girls strutting down the street in packs like an army of Valkyries, clutching their bags to their chest, huddling against the cold wind that insinuated itself between the sequins of their clothes.

But alas, the club was invariably a disaster — the music was too loud and I couldn't understand anything. We walked in, hunting for girls and free champagne, and ended up back in our dorms, alone and drunk on tonic with traces of gin. I would wake up with a stinking hangover and an overwhelming feeling of self-pity, thinking I was a willing victim in a wicked system that preyed on minimum-wage earners.

That morning Fatty Boy took some concoction containing atropine and squeezed it directly into his eyeballs to induce 'topical hallucinations' as he called them. He pulled down his lower eyelid and squirted this clear gel underneath. In fifteen minutes, the charming, middle-class pupils lining up for breakfast had all acquired tentacles. 'Sometimes,' he assured us, 'they all swim around the tables like in a big fish tank, while we're here behind the counter dishing out lamb with mint sauce.' That morning, it was octopuses — and he seriously believed he was serving breakfast to a coterie of sea creatures. Worse, he was so high he maintained the microwaved crap we served them was actually rather tasty.

My hangover hadn't fully evaporated when I got a phone call from home — it had been a while. Renato sounded spent, distant: 'I saw a West Ham match the other day — you know the ones with the crossed hammers? And I wondered … is it because over there they're all hammerers?' By 'hammerers' he meant low-skilled factory workers who do the heavy lifting but can't be trusted with the complex stuff. In his mind, English factory workers were a cross between hooligans and minor Celtic deities: blond, with shoulders the size of tanks and Saint George's crosses tattooed on their chests, donning horned helmets and blue overalls emblazoned with crossed-hammer crests. To him it was all one big Britannic hodgepodge — Gunners and trade unions, Hammers and Labour, hooligans and workers' rights. 'If I had shoulders like those,' he coughed, 'I'd still be strutting through this world like I owned the fucking place.'

And there was indeed a kind of rugged vibrancy, a feistiness I sensed in people here. On Sunday mornings I'd often see kids playing football with their forty-something dads in the park — they'd scuffle in the mud like wild boars for hours, and it occurred to me that mud was like the mortar that held this nation together. Running and tumbling in that soft dark soil saturated with rain was like performing a sacrament. It toughened you up.

When I played football as a kid and someone kicked me in the nuts, or the ball hit me in the stomach, and I curled up in pain on the dusty pitch (we've got dust back home, not mud), our coach would say, 'Get up, it's nothing, it's just the game pushing its way in.' That stayed with me, and I believe that's how I learnt to play: the game just pushed its way in. It was the same over at the steelworks, except there 'the game' pushed its way in with drops of molten steel that burned holes in your thighs. Where I grew up, the game forced its way into you one way or another; it broke you in, and it hurt. As our coach, who'd been made redundant from the steelworks, used to say: it hurts, but it'll pass, and that's how you toughen up. And there I was, in England, sitting on a bench like a lemon, watching kids kick the ball and tackle their dads and curl up in the mud if they fell too hard, and I was jealous of that mud, of their joy, of their pain that was just the game pushing its way in.

Soon, however, I'd meet someone who'd played their fair share of games in life. Gerald was retired and had a few health problems, but he still worked at the summer camp canteen from time to time. He was friends with the gardener, an old hippie who spent his days kneeling by the flower beds, his hands forever poking about in the rich, fertile English soil — sometimes we'd strike up a conversation about bluebells or hydrangeas. Gerald was also friends with Mark, the maintenance guy, who had an amazing workshop with hundreds of tools, all perfectly labelled, where I often went when I felt homesick.

On the surface, Gerald was a stinky old goat — but beneath that bulging belly, beneath his thick white brows and his watery, bloodshot eyes lay the soul of a poet. He used to be a radio actor. He'd started young, when he was in the army: after the war the RAF packed him off to occupied Germany to grace the Teutonic airwaves with his deep English baritone. Later, as a civilian, he had worked on countless radio dramas and had even been in a few theatre plays. On his fiftieth birthday, however, a blood clot clogged a vein in his brain and left him in a coma. They saved him by the skin of his teeth, but they had to remove part of his brain; you could still see where a portion of his skull was missing. The summer camp where I worked hired him as a temp during peak times, meaning he worked a few weeks in July and August, and survived on benefits the rest of the year.

I took an instant liking to him because I love old people, even when they're as filthy as he was. I only ever saw him wear one T-shirt the entire time he worked at the canteen: as the weeks went by, I watched the crusty sweat rings that mushroomed under his armpits slowly but inexorably expand downwards. I was often stationed next to him behind the counter, serving zombie-like kids who shuffled along the meat-and-two-veg assembly line at dinner. As per our contract, interactions with the pupils were effectively limited to 'cheers', 'you're welcome', 'my pleasure'. But boy, did he say them well. His voice was something else — deep, husky, intimidating. He could effortlessly climb up and down the entire male vocal range from tenor to bass, and the ladle would even move in sync with his endless modulations in an all-out theatrical performance. He'd start off on in a neutral tone and rhythm (my pleasure, my pleasure) then suddenly speed up (pleasuremypleasuremypleasure), and then slow it right down again, dragging out every syllable, whenever a nice-looking girl approached the counter (myyyyyyy pleeeaaasuuuure, doll!). Back to neutral again (my pleasure). Deep quivering bass (myy pleeaasure). Curt, clipped, military (My. Pleasure!). Defiant, sarcastic (my … pleasure). Hurried (mypleasure). Doubtful (my pleasure?). Destructive (my fucking pleasure!).

He really was a creepy old man and the kids were genuinely

afraid of him, but we kitchen assistants were in hysterics at his performances. Once, after our shift, I told him that even the way he handed out cutlery belonged on a stage, and he replied that he'd been one of the most celebrated radio actors of his time. He was particularly fond of Shakespeare's sonnets, he added. So I went to a second-hand bookshop — seemingly ubiquitous in English towns, generally owned by jovial couples so old they are practically part of the furniture — and I bought a copy of the *Sonnets*. The following day I asked him to recite a few poems for me and he obliged, treating me to a masterful performance. He wiped his forehead with his cruddy T-shirt, exposing a rosy, hairy belly, and he was off:

> Who will believe my verse in time to come,
> If it were fill'd with your most high deserts?
> Though yet, heaven knows, it is but as a tomb
> Which hides your life and shows not half your
> parts.

I gave him a standing ovation and started calling him Maestro, which he was exceedingly pleased about, seeing as everyone else treated him like a leper. He even offered to teach me how to read iambic pentameter. I went along with it for a while, but then had to stop because the rest of the gang thought I'd gone bonkers too: I was spending hours reading poems and neglecting our usual afternoon pastimes (pints, pool, and darts).

Not that going to the pub was a burden — far from

it. Sometimes I'd sit at the counter and lecture the poor
bartenders: 'Where am I from, you ask? I'm from a steel town
that makes 108-metre-long rail tracks. We're talking 108
metres of pure steel here — not pots and pans, my friends.
Tracks as long as a football stadium. Not impressed yet, are
you? Listen — you know the Old Trafford, right? A true gem,
one of the Seven Wonders of the World, like the pyramids
and Samantha Fox — and we can all agree on that. Well, the
Old Trafford measures just under 105 metres. 105 metres of
grass, whereas where I come from, we make 108-metre-long
steel bars. Picture that: 108 metres of unbroken, polished steel,
smooth as a woman's thighs. Not exactly the kind of stuff you
find down the local market, see what I mean? Half of Europe's
trains run on those tracks — including yours, my friends. And
I'll tell you something else — and then I expect all of you here
to buy me a pint: do you know who keeps things running at
these world-class steelworks the likes of which you won't find
anywhere else on the continent or the British Isles? A welder,
plumber, and all-round maintenance genius who brushes his
teeth with a brush grinder, shaves with a welding torch and
fries bacon and eggs on steel cylinders straight out of the forge.
And this working-class hero, ladies and gentlemen, is my dad.
So there you have it. Pint, please.' And when I told them of
how my dad could lift rail tracks longer than the Old Trafford
with one hand, my associates didn't bother quibbling over the
minutiae of my working-class tales and promptly reached for
their wallets.

But I'd been skipping my daily pilgrimage to the pub for

days now. Even Tim's dad, who worked as a bus driver, had been asking about me. He was worried because he'd spotted me outside the town's library more than once, and I was no longer considered 'a regular' at the bar. I knew all too well how fathers fret over the younger generations straying from the rightful path, lured away by a shady library: I had no intention of replicating the trials and tribulations of my teenage years in Italy here in the UK. And it transpired that Renato's Rules applied here too: don't be a grass, don't be a scab — Tim's dad was forever telling us — don't trust those toffs, etc. I was ecstatic: bloody hell, my dad was right, The Rules really were the same! I wonder if they can't stand Pisans either? I felt the whole world was one big working-class family, and that made me happy.

That said, even though I stuck to The Rules, getting sloshed in the pub every day was beginning to lose its shine for me. I wanted to improve my English and to experiment with more complex sentences than the usual expletives. I'd even signed up for a course to help me prepare for the First Certificate in English, but I really needed a TV to improve my oral comprehension — sadly I couldn't afford one, let alone the extortionate fee for a TV licence. I mentioned it to Ross one day, and, as ever, our team leader was happy to help a friend in need.

'You want a TV?' he said. 'Not a problem, mate — I know a bloke who's got a basement full of TVs!'

'He's not stealing them, is he?'

'Stealing? Jesus — no. Who do you take me for? He bought

them. From the guy who stole them.'

'Oh. That's all right then, I guess.'

In the end Ross got me a free TV, on condition that I put my improved English to use by helping him write yet another complaint letter to Durex — they'd all seen me reading Shakespeare, so there was really no excuse. I picked up a notepad and started writing. The problems, sadly, persisted. Yes, the complimentary 'Zebra' condoms they'd sent him did indeed fit, and yes he'd already sent them the barcode on the faulty condom pack so they could communicate it to the factory over in China which was supposed to test the remaining condoms in that lot to check for other faults. And it's great we're all contributing to improving product quality and brand image, but Pam was a fucking mess in the three weeks she didn't get her period after the condom broke, and who's going to refund him for that? And now there was another problem: the 'Zebras' gave off a smell of burnt tyres during intercourse and that put Pam off the whole business, and didn't they have another heavy-duty, fire-resistant product that didn't smell like a bloody tyre factory. Also (I added) those fumes can't be good for you, please send money ASAP for urgent pulmonary and respiratory tract diagnostic checks ('Pulmo — what?' 'Trust me, Ross'). Yours faithfully, Ross.

That was Ross for you. He was a brilliant supervisor, in the sense that when you needed him at work he was nowhere to be found, but if you were seriously struggling he'd find a way to get you out of trouble. And unlike most supervisors he was on our side, not on the boss's side. Ross, in short, was one of us, and he had no ambitions to climb up the ladder.

Not that he stood a chance — his life was a train wreck. As a child, he'd had the living daylights knocked out of him by bullies because he was so small, so he started practising karate to keep the bastards at bay. Ross never took anything seriously and talked about sex in a derogatory, chauvinistic manner — he was always on about a performance-boosting technique he'd developed himself, christened 'the bunny shuffle', and other such unspeakable acts that would only offend your delicate ears, so I'll spare you the details. At times, however, he could be extremely kind and affectionate. When I knocked on his door in the morning he always looked a bit the worse for wear — whether it was booze or drugs or a fight, those dark circles spoke volumes. But he'd still bend over backwards to help you out.

He almost made me cry once, that son of a gun. There were no books in his room aside from football memoirs — the Red Devils, Eric Cantona (who also featured in a poster hanging over his bed), Cass Pennant, John King's *The Football Factory*. Then he dug out an old volume bulging with musty pages: it chronicled the lives of Black Country miners who'd lost everything during the miners' strikes. One of these destitute families had moved to the countryside after the father lost his job and went to work at his brother's farm. Soon, however, the brother lost his farm because of outstanding debts and some land-tenure legal quagmire, and both families ended up living in a caravan.

The journalist who wrote the book interviewed the

two brothers, the miner and the farmer. The miner had five children. The youngest — recounted the author — was just a baby, crying in his twelve-year-old sister's arms. That baby was called Ross. The same Ross who now stood in front of me and handed me the book with tears in his eyes: read it, he said, and I understood then why Ross was so lenient a supervisor. He was a loser who played the tough guy, forever getting into fights — he'd sooner get beaten to a pulp than run away like a coward, because that was the working-class ethic he'd been raised in: never run from a fight even if you don't stand a chance of coming out of it in one piece. As a result, he was forever clobbering and getting clobbered for no apparent reason, especially on weekends. He was a loser, but his heart was in the right place.

Scrawny as he was, at sixteen he ended up working as a construction labourer on a building site — and one day those bastard colleagues of his tied him up to the scaffolding poles, for a laugh. 'Those fuckers crucified me', he joked. In Italy we call scaffolding poles 'Innocenti tubes' after the guy who first came up with the idea of using steel poles instead of timber. I pictured this helpless kid, his legs dangling from the far-from-innocent scaffolding.

It was during a slow week when there were no kids at the summer camp that Ross told me his crucifixion story. We'd all been redeployed to help Mark with the odd maintenance job, and were busy repainting railings, classrooms, and our beloved canteen, where Ian chucked buckets of white waterproof paint on the walls, listening to gangsta rap. After six hours of painting, we'd all cram into Ian's old red Vauxhall Corsa and find some empty parking lot to do donuts in. Ian was the only one with a car in the gang, which surprised me initially, coming from a country like Italy where everyone and their dog owns a car. That said, I found you didn't really need one in the UK because public transport was actually quite reliable, and a car was no use if you wanted to go out drinking anyway.

At any rate, Ian had this Vauxhall Corsa. Sadly the starter motor was now shot, and that wasn't even the main problem. How, you're probably wondering, could someone like Ian — a constant drain on the public purse, the scourge of social services — afford a car? Good question. The local branch of the Dorset Police Force was wondering precisely the same thing.

It's a long story: Fatty Boy explained that Ian had 'really fucked up', meaning he'd recently been stopped by the police and had given them his real name and address. ID cards, I learnt, are not a thing in the UK. You don't even have to have your driving licence on you when you drive! They just take your word for it, which I found hilarious. So anyway, Ian fancied himself a descendant of the Kray twins but was really just a moron, so instead of telling the police he was Merlin the Wizard or Gandalf the Grey or what have you, Ian gave them his real name and address. A rather unfortunate call as it happens, since the red Vauxhall Corsa we badass kitchen assistants cruised around town in was — you guessed it — stolen.

To top it all off, the old banger wouldn't start anymore and we absolutely had to remove it from the car park by our dorms where it currently languished. Ross went cap in hand to Mark the maintenance guy and begged him on Ian's behalf to help us get rid of the car before the police found it. Mark grumbled a bit and told Ian he was a twat, but then agreed to help — he'd got into a few scrapes himself in his younger days. He sat in the car, unscrewed the dashboard panel, pulled out two wires and bang! The engine started purring again. 'Ian, you stupid bastard — that's the last time I get you out of trouble. And now off with you lot and get this bloody wreck out of town.' So we did.

We thought that was the end of it. For a few days we laid low, avoiding fights and weed and pills. Ross, meanwhile, had acquired a minion who further elevated the cultural level of the gang: Alfred ended up working at the summer camp having dropped out of university after suffering a nervous breakdown. He was once a gifted Classics student, but he'd drunk so much that his command of the English language had degenerated. His grunts resembled those of a tanked-up Viking who'd just come ashore looking for a good pillage.

But alas, Alfred wasn't the only addition to the team: the managers had infiltrated our gang with a new head chef. We'd been dreading his arrival for a while. He was a bony, sixty-something bloke from South Africa with snow-white hair and blue eyes, and rumour had it that he was very good friends with the director who lived in the creepy mansion on the hill, surrounded by dead trees. He descended upon us like a Biblical plague, bringing repression into our ranks. And bad luck. And the police. Oh, and he stank of rotten fish.

But let's not get ahead of ourselves. The South African chef was a sinister, aloof kind of guy and we all disliked him from the word go. On his first day he got all the kitchen staff together and gave us a little speech — order, discipline, punctuality, blah blah blah. 'Enough fucking around,' he added, at the end. On that, Ian walked in, late as usual, and let out a majestic fish-and-chips-scented belch that left everyone speechless for a few seconds — after which we burst out laughing. The head chef let it slide, pretending not to hear, but he frowned and started barking out orders left right and centre. I was tasked with peeling the potatoes, which was actually not that hard because I just had to chuck the spuds into an infernal machine and press 'ON': after a while, the miniature cement mixer lined with blades spat the huge tubers back out, all nice and clean, ready to get boiled to within an inch of their life before a cursory foray into the oven. I tried to object that potatoes had to be blanched for a few minutes only and then properly roasted on a tray (à la John Silver), otherwise they'd go all soggy, but I was reminded not to get ideas above my station.

Then we had to offload a fresh batch of supplies from a van, consisting mostly of disgusting ready-made concoctions packed full of potato starch and E numbers. As the South African chef bent over to read a label on one of the boxes, Ian (who was listening to an Arsenal match on his earphones, and perhaps fancied he was about to kick a decisive penalty) took a running start and headed for the boss's protruding buttocks. For a second I thought he was going to kick him so hard the boss' spine would just peel off nice and neatly like deboning a fish. But he stopped just an inch shy of the boss's rear. The chef must have sensed Ian's foot whisking through the air though, because he turned, surprised, only to find my associate perfectly composed, whistling Bob Marley's 'I Shot the Sheriff'. He let it slide again.

The following day he reported us to one of the managers, who gave us a generic talking-to along the lines of 'do as you're told and don't make me escalate this to the big boss over at Cthul Manor'. Ten minutes later, however, the chef himself subjected us to a blistering tirade: we were a bunch of chavs, the dregs of society, the scum of the earth — where he was from people like us would serve food to inmates not kids, and so on and so forth. That evening, he added, he was going to play bridge with the director, and he had a good mind to ask him to fire us all.

Perhaps he didn't know any better, but Friday afternoon is a suboptimal time to piss off a gang of rogue kitchen assistants. That night Ian and Fatty Boy came back trolleyed from the pub, broke into the sports equipment shed and picked up a couple of the airguns the kids used for target practice. Cthul Manor sat right on top of the hill overlooking the sports grounds: the boys ran up to the house and hid behind some trees, then took aim — a window each. In the space of ten seconds, the glass panes had all but shattered. For a brief moment the lights came on — Fatty Boy thought he could make out a strange silhouette (was it an octopus?) at one of the windows, but the vision quickly disappeared.

He wasn't one to get too bothered by the sudden appearance of an anthropomorphic cephalopod though – that pill-popping rascal had seen far worse in the club at 2am. British working-class youths in general, it must be said, were seemingly immune to the kind of supernatural paranoia that afflicted yours truly: the two snipers calmly replaced the airguns in the shed and walked back to our dorms. After another couple of Stellas they were out for the count, oblivious to the piercing sound of rapidly approaching sirens.

The morning after our heroes' 'target practice', the police came back looking for the culprits — but found themselves in the middle of an impromptu theatrical performance instead. Hearing the sirens and sensing trouble ahead, Gerald sprang into action. The filthy old actor began reciting his beloved Bard: 'Whether 'tis nobler in the mind to suffer / the slings and arrows of outrageous fortune, / or to take arms against a sea of troubles,' he bellowed, holding up a manky old trainer in lieu of Yorick's skull. He went on crunching verses as if he'd just got a shot of adrenaline straight into his injured brain, and threw in a bit of Shelley and a couple of passages from *Frankenstein* for good measure.

The officers were completely stunned. Our associates, meanwhile, climbed out of a window and legged it across the rugby pitch just as Gerald lobbed his manky trainer over the dorm roof and then disappeared with surprising alacrity. Eventually, the officers emerged from their stupor and resolved to retrieve Gerald's trainer, which was clearly an important piece of evidence (evidence of what, exactly, remained to be seen).

Unsure how to proceed, they turned to me, pointing at the offending item on the roof. I looked at their finger. Then I looked at the shoe. Then I looked all around and below the shoe. Bloody hell, it was right under my nose and I never noticed! I couldn't get my eyes off the dorm roof. It was covered in a thick layer of asbestos tiles. The fucking bastards.

If I wanted to be rude — the head chef interjected — I could be rude in my own fucking language. Why thank you, sir, I will, much obliged. And I let out a string of the finest, most creative insults and composite obscenities Tuscany had to offer, an apotheosis of lyrical profanities that once again left everyone speechless. And with good reason, for crying out loud — they made us sleep under an asbestos roof! The boss had slate tiles; the teachers insulated wood, and as for the kitchen skivvies ... well, let them eat asbestos. But you know, we were the scum of the earth and all that. I kept pointing at the roof and all the officers saw was the manky shoe (aka Yorick's skull) Gerald had thrown up there after his masterful performance — for which, incidentally, he received no applause. Philistines.

I was, in short, royally pissed off. Poorly paid, exploited, constantly watched, persecuted by Annabelle, lectured by a South African chef, ridiculed for my visits to the library, mocked and taunted by kids who didn't understand my English, pitied by my associates when I couldn't understand theirs — and now abused by police officers who didn't appreciate impromptu theatrical performances. Short of getting killed by the asbestos roof that His Lordship over at Cthul Manor saw fit to put over our heads, I'd really hit rock bottom. Enough's enough. I felt truly oppressed. And unlike the oppressed in the novels I devoured as a kid, there was no musketeer coming to my rescue. I couldn't stay there — not if I wanted to keep breathing in that dorm room. Once again, it was time to go.

But I hung around. I found it hard to fall asleep at night, so I'd taken to gulping down a few drops of the remainder of Silver's sedative in a splash of water. I stared at the ceiling: only a sliver of plaster separated me from the deadly mineral that ruined the life of so many factory workers. Then the darkness finally swallowed me. A few hours later I was back at the canteen serving line sandwiched between Alfred and Ian, pushing trays along: I'd deposit a dollop of instant mash on the side plate next to a revolting blob ambitiously labelled 'Bolognaise lasagna', then hand it to the beast to my right — Ian — who in turn would ladle out some goopy gravy.

Gerald, for his part, contributed a Shakespeare sonnet, a drop of sweat, and a spoonful of mint sauce, his gnarly thumbnail sinking in the mash as he handed the tray to the pupil. One day, the old goat was telling me about the time he'd played in a glorious adaptation of Brecht's *Threepenny Opera* in Berlin, when all of a sudden my ladle clattered to the floor as Ian very nearly toppled into the piping-hot vats of vile food. A minor setback: two police officers had tackled Ian and bent him down over the counter, his cheek sinking in the gurgling mash while they handcuffed him in front of the astonished pupils. All this fuss over a few broken windows? I wondered.

But it was far worse than that. Our friend Ian, it emerged, was suspected of robbing a loyal (wealthy) subject of the Crown, who, alas, had found himself in the path of Ian's mighty right hook. Said unfortunate subject's wallet had somehow found its way into Ian's pockets. Apparently, that constitutes larceny.

The police officers had recognised him from an e-fit when they came to investigate the broken windows, although the robbery had taken place six months before in Manchester, after which our hero had absconded. And there was more: he was also charged with car theft — the infamous red Vauxhall Corsa — and drug dealing.

The South African chef gloated, ecstatic: if it were up to him they'd lock Ian up and throw away the key. And sure enough, ten days later we were all fired. They dismissed us a few at a time, so we wouldn't kick up a fuss. In the end, we were nothing but a pain in the neck: they tolerated us while we were needed but lost no time kicking us out as soon as summer came to an end.

And the truth is that our posse of wannabe gangsters didn't protest. Once upon a time, Black Country miners used to say that if you crossed one of them you crossed them all. These days we just pocket our meagre severance package and apply for unemployment benefits. That was the end of the SKANK: the firm was no more, the gang had no real foundations, no colours to defend. We disbanded: Ian was in jail, Tim started drinking heavily. Ross was fired on his birthday, but insisted on going out to celebrate with Pam, his girlfriend. Rather squiffy already, they began arguing on the street: Pam said something and shoved him, and Ross shoved her back. A random guy who was just coming out of a nearby pub witnessed the scene and attacked Ross. Ross dodged the punch, feinted, and landed a couple of blows in rapid succession. The attacker's friends joined in, and before long the whole pub was caught up in a massive street brawl.

Not that anyone actually knew who they were pummelling or why — it certainly wasn't to defend Pam's honour or to punish an act of chauvinistic violence. These brawls are like whirlpools: if you happen to sail close enough to the edge, you'll get sucked in. Someone slaps you and you slap them back. Someone else breaks a bottle and says they'll cut you open. At that point you can't lose face with your friends, it's a matter of pride. Bring it on, then. Scholars and literary critics have written volumes about the eternal appeal of Shakespeare's work, but in the end that's all there is to it — take a look inside any working-class pub on a Friday night and you'll see it all play out: pride, fear, vengeance, jealousy. There are more things between the counter and the toilets of any Wetherspoons, my dear Horatios, than are dreamt of in your philosophy.

Back to Iron Town

Did not Hamlet say 'cursing like a scullion'? No
doubt Shakespeare had watched scullions at work.

George Orwell, *Down and Out in Paris and London*

Unemployed, homeless, and paranoid, I felt like a roving
gringo in those Western movies I watched as a kid: lost on
a desert mesa, thirsty and feverish, with filthy clothes and a
scruffy beard. This gringo only wanted one thing: to escape
the desert and get back to his iron town. I sensed something
sneaky was on my trail: I knew the idol would follow me
wherever I went. The idol was a messenger of the Entity, the
demonic corporation named Cthul Ltd, the infernal machine
that blackmailed and oppressed workers under Britain's leaden
skies, endlessly chasing them from degrading job to degrading
job. I had to run away.

I thought about the migrant labourers who had travelled
without papers on freight trains during the Great Depression
in the US, desperately looking for work in the fields, or in
the mines, or in a factory. Maybe they, too, were running
away from the horrors of Cthul Ltd. 'I ain't got no home, I'm
just a-ramblin' around / A hard-working ramblin' man, I go

from town to town.' I was part of a long lineage of migrant workers, the Entity forever breathing down our necks. Maybe every single shop in those foreign cities, every business on those high streets was actually owned by the mother of all international corporations, the despicable Cthul Ltd. The cephalopod monster, Cthulhu, Das Kapital, the Entity, the Iron Lady's ghost: they were all the same quiet, chilling spirit that enslaved generations of human beings with the mirage of gold and riches; a slimy creature hell-bent on crushing every last pocket of resistance and subjugating the whole world to its bloodthirsty logic.

My sleep was troubled by recurring nightmares and surreal fantasies, one of which seemed to offer a strange kind of hope: in it, thousands of bees defended the hive by closing in on the Entity in a pincer movement, suffocating it in a lethal embrace. In the end, the Entity lay dead, embalmed in a bundle of propolis, cobwebs and excrement.

But bees, alas, do not concern themselves with human endeavours. I couldn't think straight. In my constant struggle to escape the loathsome Entity, I found myself completely subdued, as if mesmerised. My will now entirely bent, I didn't demand rights, I didn't fight. I was a larva in all but name, looking for a job, any job — the worst kind of job.

In a trance, haunted by dark thoughts, I accepted an offer from the local job centre: the description read 'seasonal agricultural work'. I shortly found myself five miles from the coast, in a dorm full of Eastern European workers next to a large farming estate. The room reeked of vodka and feet, but pungent as that aroma was, it was a welcome respite from the putrid smell of rotting fish that haunted me.

Vodka sanitised my murky dreams too, and to avoid reading anything creepy, I dug into my copy of Margaret Powell's *Below Stairs*. I still had the codeine drops, and on one of my darkest days I gulped some down with a glass of water. Glimpsing my sunken eyes staring back at me in the mirror however, nauseous and with an acrid taste in my mouth, I finally rebelled and found the strength to empty the bottle in the communal bathroom sink. All that rotting fish nonsense, I thought, must have been the product of my disturbed imagination, likely brought about by the out-of-date codeine drops Silver had gifted me at the pizzeria. Not to mention Tim's blue pills, Fatty Boy's atropine, Ian's weed, and, most suspect of all, the copy of H.P. Lovecraft's tales that I had picked up: a devastating cocktail.

Setting down the empty bottle, I took a deep breath, tightened my belt, and shot out of the dorm like a gunslinger striding out of a saloon. The other workers were already in the courtyard, communicating in a babel of idioms from all over the world. A cool breeze cleared my head and I felt the old brazen sarcasm resurfacing on my lips. A supervisor appeared and we all climbed on his pickup — we were about to drive off when a Polish guy leapt in. His name was Jozef and his English was limited to 'Bin!' 'Stop!' 'Go!' My new colleagues pointed him out to me, and one of them tapped his finger on his forehead: 'Crazy guy!' Jozef was indeed a bit of a loon who suffered from a form of religious paranoia (I, for my part, said nothing of my own cephalopod-based hallucinations).

They split us up into teams and we started piling into the white polytunnels. Raspberry picking was very different from my previous jobs. It felt surreal; the whole setup was like some sort of *Big Brother*-style reality show. I had pictured our supervisor as a brute walking around with a pruning knife dangling from his belt, ready to gut idle labourers: instead, he was a middle-aged foreman who maintained a positively Orwellian surveillance regime and was in constant phone communication with His Lordship the Estate Owner up in his villa. The supervisor determined who'd be remaining in the feudal lord's good graces, who'd be voted out of the (green)house, and who'd be allowed back in after atoning for their sins.

We were assigned different roles. A driver manoeuvred the little green John Deere tractor between twin rows of raspberry plants, while the pickers wrecked their backs crouching down either side of the vehicle, and picked the berries following strict instructions: the best ones were for the top-quality markets, while the shrivelled or mouldy ones were destined for the jam processing plants and would be picked at a later time. Behind the John Deere walked the bin-gatherers, whose job was to collect full bins from the pickers and empty them into the trailer attached to the back of the tractor. All these operations took place under the supervisor's constant, stifling scrutiny. He patrolled the greenhouses looking for evidence of wrongdoing and establishing the appropriate punishments.

At times he stepped it up a notch, jumping in the trailer and closely examining the quality of the berries poured in from every bin. As soon as he spotted some mouldy ones that had ended up in the trailer by mistake (or by design) he'd demand to know who had filled that bin. We knew better than to name names of course, and resorted to a variety of tactics to avoid confessing. Mixing the contents of different pickers' bins before emptying them in the trailer was a well-established ruse; another option was to infiltrate Jozef among the bin-gatherers, thereby sabotaging the whole interrogation process. Once there, Jozef pretended not to understand, shouted 'Bin!' a few times, then spread his arms and invoked God's blessing upon the greenhouses.

My own personal strategy proved, as usual, rather counter-productive: I'd managed to sneak in a bin of mouldy raspberries that stank like a wet dog, and when the supervisor asked 'Whose bin is this?' I answered: 'The Master's!' correctly identifying the owner of the means of production. My riposte earned me a stern rebuke and, inevitably, resulted in my exclusion from the (green)house: I'd been voted out due to my incompetence, poor performance, and general lack of gratitude towards the Great British agro-industrial complex.

I was out, in short — jobless once again. On the plus side, since I'd binned Silver's codeine drops I was no longer haunted by the ghost of Baroness Thatcher. I was skint, homeless, and unemployed, but I knew that with a couple of weeks' work in any pub or restaurant I could scrape together enough money for a plane ticket. And if I was really careful, maybe there'd be something left over.

I got a bus back to Stonebridge, and as I walked down the high street I almost immediately stumbled upon a job vacancy.

What got my attention was not so much the 'help wanted' sign itself, but the wooden board on which it rested, displaying a badly misspelt list of Italian dishes. I went in and enquired about the post. The management welcomed me with open arms on account of the fact that I spoke the immortal language of Dante. Or, you know, that of Vialli, Zola and Balotelli.

It didn't take me long to realise that for all their bronzed skin and dark hair these guys were not Italian. Despite exclaiming *'Napule, Napule, mannaggia!'* ('Naples, Naples, goddamnit!') when he learnt my nationality, it was clear that the owner had never so much as set foot in Italy: he confessed straight away to being Turkish.

So this was one of the many less-than-authentically-Italian restaurants that seemed to have sprung up like mushrooms in the UK. My new boss explained it was the way the market worked — there just wasn't enough money in kebabs. So why not capitalise on your Mediterranean looks, pretend you're from Naples, and sell pizza and pasta carbonara to the gullible Brits? There was a certain justice to this approach, because as I soon learnt, said gullible Brits liked their carbonara with cream instead of eggs and their pizzas with pineapple, crimes against Italian cuisine serious enough to get you shot if you ever did set foot in Naples. But despite Brits preferring these bastardised versions of our national dishes, they were still attracted to the *idea* of authenticity. So, to maintain a veneer of credibility the boss had to hire some bona fide Italians from time to time.

The job spec was, in short, 'Resident Italian': what's not to like? Pop a few pizzas in the oven, dish out some spaghetti while playing the mandolin, sing 'O sole mio' or 'That's Amore' or 'Ti Amo'. There was only one problem: I'm as tone deaf as they come. The owner (whom I immediately christened 'Mannaggia') insisted on hearing me perform, then shook his head — '*Mannaggia*,' he must have thought, 'he really can't sing.' But whether you like it or not, in restaurants as in politics, clichés sell: those Brits thought Italians were all Pavarottis, and who was I to let them down?

And yet. I hated singing! The boss suggested a compromise: if I didn't want to sing, I could bloody well talk. It was unclear, however, who I was supposed to talk to … the Prosecco bottles? Last time I'd checked you needed at least two people to have a conversation. 'Just talk to me,' he said, 'and I'll answer you mozzarella and Mussolini and *mannaggia*!' 'No, sir,' says I. 'Answer me mozzarella and Vialli, Zola and Chianti. Answer me Claudio Ranieri, Leicester City's legendary manager. Answer me whatever the fuck you want but leave fucking Mussolini and Di Canio out of it.'

Deal. We shook hands, and thus ended our farcical negotiations. Needless to say, however, I did things my way. As soon as a customer walked in, I'd regale them with a string of the filthiest Tuscan profanities I could muster — ecstatic, in their minds they were transported to the palazzi of Venice, the shores of Lake Garda, or the Renaissance villas of Florence. Mannaggia, for his part, smiled and repeated his mantra: '*Mannaggia!* Vialli!' '*I soldi che c'ha meglio prenderli che cacalli!*' I'd retort ('I'd sooner have his money than have to shit it out').

It was a sort of deranged rhyming game, a grotesque literary exercise. But our affable English customers were enraptured: 'Such a musical language ...' I gave them what they wanted — a caricature — and they, in turn, *cacavano il lesso*. That is to say, er ... they rewarded me with generous tips.

Making pizzas there was a doddle: the mozzarella and all the other ingredients were all pre-sliced and frozen, you just had to defrost them — nothing like the hours I'd spend prepping all the fresh toppings in Italian pizzerias. 'Eeeaaasy', Tim would have said. Or, in the immortal words of Gerald: 'My pleeeaaasure.' Everything tasted of preservatives and artificial taste enhancers of course, but there you have it.

It was slow going, and on Saturdays I was joined by a Yemeni apprentice. An extremely likeable guy with a bright smile and a tendency to shirk work, Emir was a student looking to earn a little extra money. Mannaggia had hired him out of a sense of responsibility, or so he maintained: 'It was the charitable thing to do,' he said, 'the boy needed work.' 'And you needed someone to do the dishes,' I countered, cynical as usual.

Emir had to pretend to be Italian too — at any rate, according to our enlightened boss, we were all foreigners together, and not exactly of the whitest complexions — so I took it upon myself to initiate him into the wonders of Tuscan insults and swear words, which he was quick to put to use with Mannaggia. In the space of a few weeks he had acquired an arsenal of Italian profanities with which he graciously greeted our honourable customers: he'd write them all down in his little notebook, meticulously transliterating my obscenities into Arabic characters.

In return, he shared with me some rather baffling theories of his, according to which Italian women's tits weren't big enough, and if you wanted a girlfriend with big jugs you had to feed her 'feminine' animals. Camels — it transpired — were masculine, whereas chickens were feminine. 'Chicken breasts!' insisted Emir, 'Guaranteed to give you big boobs!'

'I don't doubt it,' I replied, 'chickens are pumped so full of hormones these days I'm sure they do give you breasts.' Emir looked puzzled, bless him.

Emir, you see, was a bit wet behind the ears. Renato would argue he needed to 'drink a few more eggs'. And while we were on the subject of chickens and eggs, I had another one for Emir's little notebook: 'Like a guy from Padua used to say: "Chicken soup and red wine, and like a king you'll dine!" Go on — transliterate that. And I bet you're quite partial to wine too, my young friend.' Emir smiled. 'Bottoms up, hey, Emir?' I mimed downing a glass of wine, he understood and duly transliterated the new phrase.

While I imparted my encyclopaedic knowledge of foul language to Emir, who should pop in but the very same two police officers who arrested Ian. I watched as they conferred with Mannaggia, but it wasn't me they were after. Apparently, another Italian waiter who had worked at the restaurant before me was in some sort of trouble with the law. One of the officers, however, had recognised me from the canteen, and his fine deductive skills led him to the conclusion that the whole thing stank. There was a faux-Italian restaurant owned by a Turk, where an actual Italian criminal used to work. There was another Italian now working in that same restaurant. The latter was a known associate of a merry gang of thugs from the summer camp, who were guaranteed to get into trouble every time they walked into a pub. Ergo, said Italian must be up to no good. Elementary, my dear Watson.

They couldn't pin anything on me, of course — but they still told me to watch out, because they'd had enough Italian crooks to last them a lifetime. And, come to think of it, people like me were thieves even when we worked, because we stole jobs from the English. Mannaggia tried to defuse the situation: 'How about a nice Italian pizza?' he enquired amiably. 'Don't mind if I do,' replied the officers. It was us immigrants they couldn't stand, they had nothing against our pizza. Two ham and pineapple pizzas on their way!

I warned Mannaggia that my shift was over, and the oven was off, and I'd already wiped the pizza counter — as a matter of fact, I was about to take off my apron. 'Leave the apron on then, like a good lad. And get the oven going, I bet it's still hot. And if the counter gets dirty you'll wipe it again — what do I pay you for, *mannaggia*?!' I obeyed, railing against the law enforcement community and God and all the saints in paradise and Odin and the whole Nordic pantheon while I was at it. I was so engrossed in my own stream of invective that I didn't notice the insulating sleeve had once again slipped off the oven handle. It was broken, and I'd told the boss it needed replacing two hundred times already.

As I went to chuck those vile pizzas in the oven — still reciting my litany of insults — I grabbed the searing hot handle and the palm of my right hand was instantly glued to the cast iron. My flesh blistered and sizzled with a terrible hiss. 'FOR FUCK'S SAKE!' I shouted, hurling the greased pizza trays across the room. I jumped up and down on the tomato-sauce-covered floor, yelling in pain. Mannaggia was mad at me for ruining the officers' ham and pineapple pizzas. Witnessing that scene, they shook their heads and left.

I ran cold water over my seared hand, looking at the pound of flesh they'd extorted from me, and it was at that point that I made an irrevocable decision. That oppressed flesh called out to me: it was my own father's flesh too, seeking revenge for the white-hot pipes that fell on his shin once, at a building site.

I swore on my pulped, blistering hand that this time I'd leave for good. But I had a few scores to settle first. Like in the good old days of 'Operation Unsealed Lips', I burst into the dining area and spouted a torrent of abuse at the astonished clientele, my seared palm — held out high for everyone to see — conferring sinister tones to my otherwise laughable English. I swore I'd tell all and write the whole sorry story of my time in the UK. I swore it on the blood of all the oppressed, wounded, and humiliated workers.

And with that oath (which replaced my original pledge of loyalty to the Queen) I was free: free from all my demons, from the ghost of Margaret Thatcher, and from sinister forces. Free to live and fight another day. That was me out. Go ahead and hang that 'vacancy' sign on the window, update the job centre's register, make room for all those entitled brats whose unparalleled work opportunities I'd stolen. See how many of them fancy a spot of toilet cleaning. Or sleeping under an asbestos roof. Or searing their hand on an oven handle that doesn't meet the most basic Health and Safety requirements. Far be it from me to hinder the professional development of the more privileged class — I wouldn't be so crass!

I shouted all this and more to the astonished customers who, embarrassed, abandoned their meals and left. Mannaggia tried to push me back into the kitchen, to no avail: I was beside myself and kept ranting and pointing at my right hand. In the end he bandaged it himself, probably so he wouldn't have to look at it anymore. He said 'I'll pay you, *mannaggia*, I'll pay you everything but shut that big mouth of yours — just tell me how much and get out!' I demanded an exorbitant sum, roughly equivalent to three months' salary, which he paid in cash without the slightest objection (not even the usual *mannaggia!*), fearing I'd report him. So I asked for more as 'redundancy pay'. He didn't bat an eyelid.

I walked away with a bandaged hand, a few extra pounds in my pocket, and not the slightest trace of anxiety in my heart — only anger and determination. Clear-headed anger, mind you: there was no more fear, I really had nothing left to lose.

———

The plane took off from Stansted airport, piercing the leaden blanket of clouds. As soon as I set foot on the tarmac at Pisa airport I felt unbearably warm and I thought the plane engines must still be on. But it wasn't the plane engines: it was just Italy. All of a sudden I felt a strong urge to see the sea and feel the warm libeccio wind on my skin, to taste schiacciata flatbreads and Livorno's traditional espresso punch. My days as a wannabe hooligan — all those 'yes, sir' and 'you fucking bastards', all those rotten-fish hallucinations — were only a distant memory now, blurry fragments of a dream. I knew it would be some time before I could smell the sea at Calafuria, leaning out of the window as the train sped south along the Aurelia. And then there'd be oak woods and heather and stone pines and Bolgheri with its towers and its tall, fierce cypresses, and then, out in the distance, my very own iron town, with its steelworks and its twin rows of stacks.

I wasn't prepared for the eerie silence that shrouded the train station in Campiglia, where I waited for my connection. Two freight wagons rusted away on a set of abandoned tracks. Passers-by walked briskly without exchanging a word, their eyes glued to the pavement. An elderly gent, the only talkative person at the station's bar, downed a glass of red wine and said to me, 'You see, lad, I'm almost full. The fact is … they should have put it up here!' he giggled, tapping his forehead. 'My mouth! They should have put it up here when I was born. Either that, or given me a bigger belly. The way it is, with my mouth just above my chin, I fill up in no time. If it was on my forehead there'd be room for a few more glasses, hey?' He winked. He looked scruffy and stank of booze. I glanced at the other punters — there was a palpable atmosphere of anger. Some swore under their breath, others blamed the younger generations, a small group was punching slot machines in a corner.

I'd travelled thousands of miles, and for what? Those were the same scenes I'd see in English pubs. I stepped out into the cool sea breeze and looked up towards my Piombino, set against the glorious outline of Elba — the iron island — shimmering like a treacherous mirage beyond the steel plant stacks. But there was something missing: the heavy smoke that forever cloaked the docklands and the coal depot and the blast furnace, all the way down to the Cotone housing estates, was gone. The stacks were still there, dwarfing even the Diaccioni tower blocks, but the air was clear — white-washed almost. The sky I remembered was gloomy, a dark shade of grey even in the brightest of days. Astonished, I stared at that faded, empty sky — empty like the train carriage I finally climbed into. One stop and I was home.

I got off the train and started walking along the tracks, safe in the knowledge that everything would be exactly as I'd left it — isn't that what they say about small towns, that nothing ever changes? And sure enough, there was Quattr'etti staring at the tracks, lost in thought. He was an old factory worker, a friend of my dad's. When he saw me he jumped up and gave me a hug, then bought me a glass of red wine at the train station bar. The wine was still the same, and the punters. But the atmosphere was different; there was an air of generalised despondency about the place. Quattr'etti himself hadn't changed one bit: skin and bones, gaunt, big nose. I asked him how he was doing. 'How am I doing …' he replied. 'I'm doing like a retired factory worker. How about yourself?'

'I'm just back from the UK.'

'Ah. I've worked abroad too, you know?'

'Where?'

'BMW. Munich. Bastard cold. Treated us like animals — only the Turks and the Greeks helped us out.'

'So it was cold, hey?'

'Cold you say? Listen — I had to be out of the house shovelling snow around the car at 5 am so I could leave at 6 to go to work.'

'Shit …'

'I got mixed up once and cleared someone else's car …'

'Bet you were swearing like a whole fucking army of truckers!'

'Swearing, kicking tyres, you name it …'

He cracked a smile that instantly died on his lips. Something was gnawing at him. 'Is everything all right?' I asked.

'Nothing's all right these days — just take a look around. Look at these young people, their faces … what do you think they survive on? Their old man's pension … or what's left of it. The lucky ones work as waiters three months a year. But those steady factory jobs, three shifts a day all year round … they're gone now. They've packed it all up.'

'What do you mean packed it all up?'

'I mean they shut it down. The blast furnace's off – didn't they tell you?' he said, then downed the rest of his wine. Only then I realised that the reason the sky over Piombino looked so clear from the train station in Campiglia was that the blast furnace wasn't puffing up smoke anymore, and neither were the flue gas stacks.

'But … that's impossible … it's been there for over a century!'

'Don't I know it! I'm the one who kept it running, fed it coal day in day out, fed it like it was my own child. Worked at the steelworks for thirty years — did you know there were five coaches carrying workers from Follonica to Piombino every day, three shifts a day? I kept it alive, that place; I fed it and it fed me too, and my daughter, paid for her studies … Knuckle down, I'd say to her when I left for the night shift. Knuckle down and then pack up your things because there's no more work here … So many times I told her … Ah, but you should have seen that plant … the metal workers … artists, they were. Yes sir, artists — that was true craftsmanship. You should have seen how they poured a casting of molten iron! Then straight to the rolling mills … and then my job was to check all parts of the beam — head, web, and foot. I'd file the heads nice and smooth and remove mill scale with a brush grinder. And if I found a crack or a fissure, I'd send the faulty beam back. Nothing got past me, you hear me? And then one day … shut it all down, they said. Just like that. And the furnace, bless his heart, took months to cool off … he died a slow death. They say he's still warm. And I … it makes me cry to think that … oh sod it. But I mean, they didn't have to … they could have fed him just enough coke to keep him going …'

I didn't know what to say. Since they privatised Italsider, the steelworks had been bought and resold at every turn — the plant must have changed hands three or four times already. What will the two thousand remaining workers do now, I wondered? 'I'll tell you what those poor sods will do now,' continued Quattr'etti, as if he'd read my mind. 'Fuck all is what they'll do! Will you believe they just shut it down like that? A plant that supported thousands of families, Europe's best railway tracks were made here, in Piombino ... the second-largest steelworks in the whole of Italy, only Taranto's was bigger ... and our stuff was the highest quality in Europe, end of. Shut it all down, they said, you buy railway tracks from China these days, they said. Your children can work in restaurants or beach clubs or babysit. Or they can go abroad ... I mean, is this what people around here are supposed to do? Fight over the crumbs that fall from the tourists' tables on Elba?'

Tears streamed like molten iron from the blast furnace that still burned inside Quattr'etti's chest. 'My daughter left for Berlin yesterday ... and since then I've been sat here at the train station bar ... drinking and looking at the tracks I made with my own two hands ... 108 metres of pure steel, and all so she could get away faster.'

He kept sobbing like a child and I didn't know what to do. I was embarrassed; I hadn't expected such a depressing homecoming. Every morning on my way to school I'd walk past the bus stop where the steel mill workers waited for their coach, and if it was early enough I'd catch them there, waiting, and I'd wave, and they'd wave back: 'Look, it's Renato's boy!' they'd say. 'You study hard, son, study hard!' And I did, and I learnt to use metaphors, and I learnt that the Romans called the island of Elba 'Ilva', like the steel company.

'So ... they named the island after the steelworks?' asked Quattr'etti. 'No ... the other way round, Quattr'etti, the other way round. But anyway, the point is, we've been melting metals around here since the Romans. Back then Elba had the largest iron ore deposits in the whole of the Mediterranean ... and all those minerals seeped into place names too — Piombino: the lead town; Portoferraio: the iron harbour. Hard as steel, our place names. Did you know that in 1943 the plant workers rebelled and built their own bombs and managed to sink the ships of the Nazi troops stationed in town? Nazi occupation, strikes, you name it — the stuff they've been through; they chained themselves to the rail tracks once, the best rail tracks in Europe, like you said, Quattr'etti, 108 metres of the best steel you'll ever see, colossal beams that never buckled! Please don't cry, Quattr'etti, or I'll cry too ... and even before they built the Piombino steelworks there were metal casting workshops all over the area: the Archduke's foundries in Follonica and Valpiana, a little mining village by Lake Accesa, little furnaces in Rocca San Silvestro ... I mean, you can't go for a walk in the woods around here without stumbling on a medieval mining village, or an Etruscan foundry, or even a fucking Neolithic portable clay furnace — like when they were done melting they'd pack it all up and move a mile further down and start melting iron again for fuck's sake, am I right? I've been studying our history all my life, Quattr'etti, and believe me when I tell you we've been melting coal and iron for nine thousand years in a row round these parts, and just like that they want to shut down the steelworks? And if the people have no iron, so fucking what, let them eat cake — right, Quattr'etti? Jesus Christ. I go away for a year and everything goes to pot? What do I tell my English mates now? Rail tracks longer than the Old Trafford, I'd told them. Bloody hell. I turn my back for one second and they pack up the steelworks! And now that I'm back, everyone else is leaving?'

Quattr'etti squeezed my shoulder: 'Come now, son. Don't you start crying now. We used to complain about pollution you know, from the plant. And now the air's clean we all miss that big fat cauldron ... And anyway it's just like you said,' he continued, to cheer me up. 'It's just like you said: nine thousand years ... but enough of that, they're not worth the steam off my piss these people ... they said a bloke from Algeria bought the plant, now they're saying it's the Chinese, or the Indians, or was it the cowboys ... they can send in the fucking Martians for all I care. The truth is no one will come, we're all alone here, and soon we'll be forgotten.'

I listened to him with a lump in my throat, wishing I hadn't come home. At least back in the UK I didn't know about the steelworks, because Renato didn't tell me — he was ashamed perhaps, as if it was his fault somehow that things had gone to pot. But there I was, at the train station, staring at Quattr'etti's furrowed brow. 'So what do we do now?' 'No idea,' he answered. 'You can always go back to the UK. Me? I'll stay here, drink my red wine, and when I see another kid leave — because they all leave, for Paris, or London or Berlin or Barcelona — good on you, I'll say to them, jump on a train and run away from this country that's gone to shit. But as the train whisks you away, ta-tum, ta-tum, ta-tum, remember that every 108 metres you clock, you're on a rail track built here in Piombino by the best metal workers in the world, and if you can run away on these fancy superfast trains now, it's only thanks to your dads, who fed coke to the blast furnace with just the right amount of oxygen and technical gases and then moulded and filed the steel just so, and let's hope these tracks that take you away now will bring you back one day, and that we'll still be around to welcome you. Can you smell the steel billets and the wire rods on us? Can you? That stuff got in deep under our skin. We were the tracks you ran on when you were little … now let's at least hope what we built can buy you a chance away from this empty sky.'

Again, that lump in my throat. I could smell freshly cut iron on Quattr'etti, I could smell the wire brush grinder languishing in a drawer. My father's smell. Quattr'etti talked too much, like all lonely old people when they find someone who'll listen to them.

'Truth be told, it was a hellish job. People got sick, hurt themselves, died. It was a shit way to earn a living, but it was the only way around here — and now we don't even have that anymore. Better than what they have you do these days, though. All the bullshit they come up with to get you to work for nothing … hamsters on a fucking wheel is what you are! Bloody hell. Round and round you go like circus animals. Us, we don't get to go anywhere anymore — and we get pretty cranky at best. But we stay here. There's this story doing the rounds … it's probably bullshit but anyway, they say they want to dismantle the furnace and build it back brick by brick in Brazil, next to an iron mine. I figure there'll be factory workers there just like us. Another Piombino, by the ocean — well bugger me! I'll tell you what. Before I die I want to take a trip to Brazil. You want to stare at all those fine buttocks in Rio, you'll say. Fuck do I care about that. I want to go see my blast furnace that they rebuilt over there, see if they run it proper. And if they don't, I'll show them how it's done, teach them a lesson or two, you know? Oh, I'll teach them all right, chase them all the way to the bloody Andes if I have to! Because you have to pass on the knowledge to those that come after you, to the next generation, and you have to teach them right. And you, with all your fancy words and your metaphors, don't you forget that steel fed you and clothed you and paid for your studies, so it did. Now you show those bastards … tell our story, tell it like it is … the parents are done, you're going to have to be the parents now, you hear me? And I'll tell you something else … go to your dad, go, quick, and see how he's doing, I saw him the other day and he was walking funny, almost bent over he was … there's something the matter with him.'

All of a sudden, I felt all those pub fights, all those blabbering beer-fuelled conversations crashing down on me like a wave. Broken glass on the streets on a Sunday morning, black eyes and bruises (on women, mostly), teenage bullies, victimised Pakistanis, marginalised toilet cleaners, overbearing supervisors: all the injustices I'd witnessed hit me like a punch to the gut, and I could feel them all on my own skin, I could feel them on my wounded hand, as if my body was itself a blast furnace where all this abuse fused into one single blob of steel, melted by the tears of an old factory worker. And that blob of molten steel and blood in my chest hurt like hell. It still hurts.

I hurried home and found a few people gathered in the garage. My mum was there, together with three neighbours, all intent on disconnecting a pipe that linked two old wine barrels to a pump: the contraption functioned as an autoclave for our plumbing system. It was one of my dad's inventions, a home-made contrivance that he alone knew how to operate.

Quietly, I came up close behind them and blurted out: 'So, what are you up to here?' Mum jumped up and hugged me: 'You've changed so much! I barely recognised you!' The neighbours hugged me too. They were all retired now, they said — there was no more work down at the mill. And this gaggle of pensioners stood there, baffled, trying this and that spanner, without success. 'Why can't Dad take care of this?' I whispered to my mum.

The others, meanwhile, were apparently incapable of disconnecting a simple pipe fitting. I started laughing, remembering how Renato enjoyed playing tricks on us 'potterers', and I warned them: 'That nut's not a standard one — Dad made it himself at the mill's workshop, and I bet it's a reverse-thread nut, just the thing to fool us novices.' I picked up a spanner, and with a quick, neat, clockwise twist (the way you'd usually tighten a nut) I disconnected the fitting. The seal loosened and a rivulet of rusty-brown water spilt onto the floor. We all laughed, all except Mum who stood in a corner, withdrawn. Then, as if getting a load off her chest, she blurted out: 'Dad can't come down to the garage. He's been unwell for a while now … bet it was all that funny stuff he breathed in at work. He didn't want to tell you, didn't want to worry you … that's why he didn't call so often. Thank goodness you're back. He's always tired these days. Go — he's resting in his armchair. Go upstairs and say hello to him.'

I ran upstairs. I wanted to tell Renato I had followed The Rules, and that The Rules really were the same in the UK, and that Tim's dad preached those ten commandments every day in the pub in between pints. If a toff calls you sir, run a mile, and so on. I wanted to tell him everything, and hug him, but the words died on my lips. I heard a harmonica play, and as I peeked into the living room I was greeted by a wind-buffeted Charles Bronson on our TV — an old Spaghetti Western. And opposite Bronson, a plaid blanket covering his hollow legs, sat another weary gringo, an old cowboy of the steelworks. Emaciated, a three-day stubble on his chin, Renato turned to look at me and coughed violently, then cracked a wonky smile à la Steve McQueen.

I could scarcely believe he was my father. Slowly, pivoting on his elbow, he swung around to face me and pulled himself up. He started fiddling with his hearing aid, producing a loud screech that obliterated the film score for a few seconds. Finally he spoke, in a barely audible voice: 'Oh, it's you … Your mum pulled a fast one on me the other day, you know. She let the priest in to bless the house. He sprinkled a few drops of water here and there with that contraption of his, then asked for money to rebuild the church steps.' He bent over his knees, coughing violently, then raised his head. 'If everyone went to Mass as often as I do, I said to him … if everyone …' He coughed again, unable to continue. I walked up to him and put a hand on his shoulder, and then I saw his eyes glimmer with the old steely determination as words gushed out of his phlegmy lungs: 'Hell, I said to him, if everyone went to Mass as often as I do,' he concluded over Morricone's violins, 'these steps of yours would be brand new, for Chrissake!'

I was in shock. So it was true, he was ill, like Quattr'etti said. My heart raced, I felt dizzy, my legs buckled — a delirious thought crept into my mind: could it be … could it be that the sinister idol had never actually lost track of me? That it had anticipated my moves even, and beaten me home? Maggie the Destroyer — with her belt of proletarian skulls, sitting astride a dragon spouting oil-refinery flames and specks of molten iron — was she really after this old factory worker? I honestly didn't know. Speechless, I leant against the armchair, holding Renato's hand. I looked at that hand, seemingly the only part of his body the disease hadn't laid waste to. It was the hand I remembered, strong but kind. I looked at my own hand, still bandaged and sore. A childhood memory came to mind: my father making a fist and challenging me to open it. I never could open it. I remembered him teaching me to use his tools — remembered my hesitating hands, his confident ones gripping a farrier rasp. I remembered seeing middle-class dads desperate to show off their DIY 'skills' — but they didn't have my father's magic touch. I watched them abuse wood or metal until their clumsy fingers went white from the effort and they let out a frustrated snort.

Renato's, by contrast, were a magician's hands. Looking at those fingers that tickled bolts loose and tightened nuts with the rugged tenderness of an awkward teenager, my tired eyelids felt heavier and heavier, and I slowly slipped into a drowsy reverie. My thoughts were sucked into a humming vortex as my mind desperately grasped for something to hold on to. I could still feel my dad's feeble pulse in my hand, yet I was surrounded by other bodies. Workers. I smelt the acrid gases of the oil refinery in Busalla, where Renato had worked under a flare stack that spouted fire like a huge dragon. I heard the racket of the steelworks in Taranto and Terni. Grey asbestos powder penetrated my lungs like it had penetrated his. Then, suddenly, I was sweating in the hot sun. My knees ached as I crouched on a black field with a vacant look in my eyes. The others around me were called Mohamed, or Arun, or Karim. When they were done picking artichokes, they'd probably end up stacking boxes in a large storing facility, or maybe they'd be whisked away by some Mafioso recruiter to another ghetto of tents and corrugated iron near a field of tomatoes.

What I couldn't see, however — beyond the bent backs of the artichoke pickers, beyond Renato's hand — was a cluster of wild beehives sheltered behind a hedge of medlars. I could hear them humming in my head. And then I saw it: protected by her guards, a queen bee had just begun her mating flight, pursued by a handful of drones. One by one the males approached the queen, their abdomens ripping open as they detached themselves from that lethal embrace. Ecstatic and hollowed out, they spiralled into the abyss. The triumphant queen returned to the hive carrying enough sperm to last her for years of egg-laying. She'd left a virgin queen and came back a deadly bride. I could feel her energy radiating through me. Like her, I trusted the worker bees would know what to do: their perseverance was my perseverance.

My trance continued: one day, joining together in a joyful dance, worker bees would surround and smother that evil creature, the Entity. In a few decades, there would be millions of migrant bee colonies, endlessly swarming across borders. Abandoned hives would be recolonised and the wild meadows, forests and mountain tops would once again be abuzz with life. New generations of worker bees would continue breaking the chains the Entity has been forging in the basements of shopping centres all over the world; nature overthrowing the tyranny of market logic which catapulted humanity out of its own species' gravitational orbit.

Maybe I wouldn't live to see that day, but I knew that day would come, and I knew I could hurry it along. I had to get it all down on paper. I knew that if I hadn't travelled I wouldn't have understood my story, or the stories of those like me. And if you can't write, then what use are a pair of delicate writer's hands? Everything I had lived through had prepared me to do it. Because what can you possibly have to say if your eyes have never seen, if your heart has never hoped or longed for anything, if your stomach's never gone hungry, if you've never felt bile corrode your guts? Because you can't fight the status quo without chestnuts in your pockets. You can't weld words together page after page, fusing nouns and screws, bolts and commas. You can't ride your memories like a bike or bounce metaphors on your toe if you spend your life navel-gazing in your own room, with ivy climbing up your legs.

If I hadn't left, I would have never have dreamt my dreams in English — the language of Shakespeare and Gerald the mad actor, of Silver the pantry pirate, and now the language of your humble narrator, too. My words are the words of bards and lost causes, of itinerant knights who fight windmills, of pilgrims who carry utopias on their backs, who work as luggage handlers or cleaners or waiters and take evening classes. The words of those who demand bread and roses, a fair salary and love sonnets.

Speaking of Shakespeare, I have news of my beloved SKANK Calibans back in the UK. Ian was released on parole and enrolled in a 'social rehabilitation' programme. He's studying towards a professional qualification and swears he'll never deal drugs again. From time to time, he delivers pizzas on his bike. Tim made good on the promise to his father to take drinking more seriously, and now manages a pub on Stonebridge's stunning bay. The old man's delighted — he spends his days parked on a bar stool clutching a pint of stout. As for Alfred, he got his life back on track: he has a girlfriend (one of the girls from the summer camp's teaching staff) and has gone back to university. Meanwhile, in Bristol, Brian works as an independent consultant for companies specialising in removing drain blockages. Kate got tired of faking a posh accent and left — not for Alicante or the Canaries, though: she went back to Belfast. Even old Long John Silver decided it was time to retire — they say he's got treasure stashed somewhere. He lives on a barge moored on Bristol's docks, which he bought with his 'hard-earned savings', as he says, and only sets foot on land to wet his whistle in a pub. He's still a citizen of the world and stranger in every place, and all he needs is a barge, a mooring, and a line. He doesn't even miss his cough drops anymore.

As for Ross, he has a very demanding job now: he works in an institution for disabled children with serious health issues. He tells me of kids who self-harm in the canteen. One bled all over him, another one tried to kill himself by jumping in a nearby ditch: Ross had to fish him out of the boggy water himself. No one could last a year in that place, but Ross keeps at it because he's a fucking fighter who looks trouble straight in the eye and knows how to take life's blows without stumbling. He may have a meltdown from time to time and wreck his room, but sooner or later he'll pull himself up, straighten Eric Cantona's photo, and get back to business.

Do you think that's a shit job? For someone who was crucified on scaffolding poles for over three hours, that job is a walk in the park, believe you me. The kids love him, and he ploughs on, like a muddy rugby player a few yards from the try line. Greetings to you, Ross, my very own working-class hero, from an Italy that you'll never see because you couldn't care less about fair Verona, or learned Padua, or whatever the news is at

St Mark's Square. You are the patron saint of pints and broken backs, of uppercuts and black eyes — your heart's as big as the Old Trafford, and if they crucify you again forgive them if you want, for they know not what they do. But don't turn the other cheek! Let them taste your right hook instead, and then tell the world — shout it with pride from your scaffolding like a mad prophet — that as you do unto the humblest of my brethren, you have done unto me. You were a friend to me, and not a day goes by that I don't remember you walking in your sports jacket with your head held high against the rain. And thank you for that TV, to which I owe a good chunk of my English — and therefore a good chunk of my income these days, as I earn a living flipping words over from the language of Shakespeare into that of Dante.

And last but not least, Gerald — my lowborn hero, who in the winter of your life still paid homage to the glowing beauty of young English roses, and lent your voice to the old poets while drops of sweat tumbled into bowls of goop and unto thy greasy T-shirt. You were our Elder, dispensing advice and potato soup, reminding us poor skivvies besieged by managers and cops in our asbestos-clad dorm that the time of life is short, and if we live, we live to tread on kings.

To every single one of you, my British mates, I owe a bit of this beggar's opera, written by an itinerant bard for an illustrious audience — a bard that even taught you a few vile metaphors in his native language, promptly transliterated into Arabic characters by a Yemeni kid. My comrades, my brothers in arms, there will always be another round waiting for us in our old pub, and a muddy football pitch for us to roll on after a nasty slide tackle. And I'm not afraid to fall anymore, because I know that there will always be a hand helping me back onto my feet on the lush hills of England. And when I am sad and dejected like a decommissioned blast furnace, through the wind and the rain, clutching my groin after life has kicked me in the nuts, though my dreams be tossed and blown, I know you'll reach out to me and tell me: it's nothing, it's just the game pushing its way in. I know I'll never walk alone.

Epilogue

Little by little, the buzzing noise faded, as did memories of my life in the UK. I opened my eyes, emerging from my stupor. I had dreamt Renato's dreams interwoven with mine, while past, present and future blended into one. In a bizarre metamorphosis, the bees had taken on a human appearance, transforming into my British associates and Renato's colleagues, from oil refineries and school canteens to steelworks and shopping centres. Then they became bees again and laid eggs which one day would swarm and form another colony. Somewhere, in a distant future, after eons of struggles, the bees would defeat the Entity.

I opened my eyes. Renato's hand was still resting inside mine. He seemed to breathe regularly now, a slow, wheezing whistle. He looked relaxed as his chest rose and sank — he was breathing from his belly, like a child. He had just gone into a coma.

A bee landed on his hand, then crawled onto mine. It paused for a while, then it whirled its wings, buzzed through the window, and it was gone.

THE END

Acknowledgements

I would like to thank Bristol's bogs and Dorset's school kitchens and canteens from the bottom of my heart for the writing fellowship they awarded me. Without their minimum-wage support, this working-class epic would never have seen the light of day.